Choosing Judaism

FELDMAN LIBRARY

THE FELDMAN LIBRARY FUND was created in 1974 through a gift from the Milton and Sally Feldman Foundation. The Feldman Library Fund, which provides for the publication by the UAHC of selected outstanding Jewish books and texts, memorializes Sally Feldman, who in her lifetime devoted herself to Jewish youth and Jewish learning. Herself an orphan and brought up in an orphanage, she dedicated her efforts to helping Jewish young people get the educational opportunities she had not enjoyed.

In loving memory of my beloved wife Sally
"She was my life, and she is gone;
She was my riches, and I am a pauper."

"Many daughters have done valiantly, but thou excellest them all."

MILTON E. FELDMAN

CHOOSING JUDAISM

LYDIA KUKOFF

"Whether we are born Jewish
or have converted to Judaism,
we are all Jews by choice."

Union of American Hebrew Congregations

NEW YORK, NEW YORK

Library of Congress Cataloging in Publication Data

Kukoff, Lydia
  Choosing Judaism.

  1. Proselytes and proselytizing, Jewish—Converts from Christianity—Biography. 2. Kukoff, Lydia. 3. Jews—California—Los Angeles—Biography. I. Title.
BM729.P7K8   296.7'1   81–10306
ISBN 0–8074–0151–X   AACR2
ISBN 0–8074–0151–1 (pbk.)

This book is lovingly dedicated to

Ben,

my husband,

and

David and Naomi,

my children,

my teachers and supporters always

and chief among my joys,

and

Louise Marella

and

Jim Marella, may his memory be for blessing,

who formed me

"If I could have invented a religion, it would be Judaism."

BERT

"I had always felt certain things, but I never knew where I belonged. I didn't know what to call myself. Now I have a name. I am a Jew."

JOANNE

Rachel

For her blood runs in my blood
and her voice sings in me.
Rachel, who pastured the flocks of Laban,
Rachel, the mother of the mother.

And that is why the house is narrow for me,
and the city foreign,
for her veil used to flutter
in the desert wind.

And that is why I hold to my way
with such certainty,
for memories are preserved in my feet
ever since, ever since.

Rachel
(Bluwstein)

Translated from the Hebrew by Naomi Nir. © by the translator, 1979, from *Voices within the Ark,* Howard Schwartz and Anthony Rudolf, eds., Avon, 1980.

"The Torah was given in public for all to see, in the open. For if it had been given in the Land of Israel, Israel would have said to the nations of the world, you have no share in it;

"Therefore, the Torah was given in the wilderness, in public, for all to see, in the open, and everyone who wishes to receive it, let them come and receive it."

FROM THE *MIDRASH*

CONTENTS

Editor's Introduction

WHENEVER you hear a group of knowledgeable Jews talking about the new Jewish sensitivity to those who have come to Judaism through conversion, the discussion inevitably turns to the work of Lydia Kukoff. Before thousands of listeners at conventions, or in one-to-one conversations with her many students, Lydia Kukoff makes a difference in the way people see themselves and their future as Jews.

We are proud to bring you Ms. Kukoff's first book, *Choosing Judaism.* It is intended for those who have already come to Judaism through conversion and those who are considering doing so. As importantly, however, it is must reading for Jewish spouses, in-laws, rabbis, educators, congregational leaders—indeed for any thinking, caring Jew.

We extend our gratitude to the distinguished Jewish teachers and leaders who added so much to this volume through their important comments and suggestions:

Mr. David Belin, Chairman of the UAHC-CCAR Task Force on Reform Jewish Outreach;

Rabbi Max Shapiro, Co-Chairman of the Task Force;

Rabbi Sanford Seltzer, Director of the Task Force;

Rabbi Leonard Schoolman, UAHC Director of Program;

Ms. Edith J. Miller, Assistant to the President of the UAHC;

Rabbis Bernard Zlotowitz, M. Robert Syme, Murray Blackman, and Steven M. Reuben, members of the UAHC-CCAR Joint Commission on Jewish Education;

Patrice Heller, David Katz, and Howard Laibson, fifth-year rabbinic students at the Hebrew Union College-Jewish Institute of Religion in New York.

As always, we are grateful to Mr. Stuart Benick, UAHC Director of Publications, for his work in bringing the book to completion.

Above all, we are grateful to Lydia Kukoff, for sharing her special brilliance and sensitivity with a generation of Jewry in need of the guidance she offers.

RABBI DANIEL B. SYME
UAHC Director of Education

Introduction

"A desire fulfilled is sweet to the soul."
Proverbs 13:19

"BLESSED are You, the Eternal our God, Ruler of the universe, who has kept us in life, sustained us, and enabled us to reach this time."

This is a blessing that Jews say at special moments in their lives. I said it for the first time when I became a Jew. With that berachah, Shehecheyanu, I expressed the thankfulness I felt at having attained a unique, personal goal. Choosing Judaism has enriched my life. Yet, because I began my Jewish life as an adult, my choice also created a challenge. I had to build a Jewish past for myself. This didn't happen overnight. At first I didn't know how my non-Jewish past—all those experiences and memories that were so much a part of me—could possibly be integrated into my Jewish present. But I devoutly hoped that I could—and would—make it happen.

So I'm writing to you, not so much to tell you about

Judaism (many books have already been written about that), but to talk about Judaism-by-choice. I want to tell you about some of the feelings and experiences that I and many others just like me have had since our first Jewish moment. You are now beginning a process, that of building your life upon a set of premises which are entirely different from any you might have expected. Having struggled with the same set of circumstances—and having lived through it—I hope my thoughts will both offer you support and enable you to take some short cuts on your way to full participation in Jewish life. And, if you happen to be a Jew by birth, I hope you will better understand the challenges, the problems, the hopes, the dreams, and the fulfillment of those of us who have come to Judaism through conversion.

C. S. Lewis once said: "Friendship is born at that moment when one person says to another: What! You, too? I thought I was the only one!" If Lewis was correct, you are about to make a host of new friends, men and women who previously shared your doubts and anxieties, yet who today are living Jewish lives in a rich and meaningful fashion. They will attest to the fact that being a Jew *is* possible. It is part of a process, a process in which you are not alone.

Some Interesting People
in History
Who Chose Judaism

1.	*Abraham*	The first Jew.
2.	*Ruth*	The great-grandmother of King David.
3.	*Aquila and Onkelos*	Two famous translators of the Bible. Aquila translated the Bible into Greek, Onkelos into Aramaic.
4.	*Flavius Clemens*	Nephew of the Roman emperor Vespasian and himself a Roman consul during the first century C.E.
5.	*Kahina*	The Berber queen of the Aures region of Algeria. According to Arab authors, Kahina and her entire tribe converted to Judaism. In a major victory against Arab invaders, she took many prisoners, one of whom she adopted. This adopted "son," Khalid, betrayed

Kahina who died while leading troops in battle about 700 C.E.

6. *King Bulan of Khazaria*

According to tradition, King Bulan instituted Judaism throughout his kingdom about 740 C.E. After a religious debate on the relative merits of Judaism, Christianity, and Islam, Bulan favored Judaism and he and his servants adopted it. Bulan and his successors were tolerant of Moslems and Christians, but the Jewish kingdom was finally destroyed by a coalition of Russians and Byzantines.

7. *Bodo-Eleazar*

Bodo was a French churchman in the court of King Louis the Pious. In 838 C.E., during a trip to Moslem Spain, Bodo converted to Judaism and adopted the name Eleazar.

8. *Obadiah*

Obadiah, born with the Christian name Johannes, came from a noble family in twelfth-century southern Italy. As a young man, he heard the story of an archbishop, Andreas, who came to Judaism after a lifetime in the church. Johannes (Obadiah) was so moved by this account that he converted to Judaism. He wrote pamphlets urging religious people to return to Judaism, was imprisoned, and threatened with death as a result. Fortunately, Obadiah escaped and made his way to Baghdad. For the remainder of his life, he wrote, visited Jewish communities in Syria, Palestine, and Egypt, and notated synagogue music. His manuscripts in this latter realm are the oldest discovered to date.

9. *Catharine Weigel*

She was the wealthy widow of a Polish merchant and a member of the Cracow city council. In 1530, after converting to Judaism, she was accused of "Judaizing" and recanted. Nine years later, at the age of 80, she was once again accused of missionary activity. This time she refused to recant and was burned at the stake.

10. *Lord George Gordon*

Gordon entered the English Parliament in 1774. Some ten years later, he became interested in Judaism. Though he was rebuffed by the London rabbinical authorities, he persisted and was circumcised outside of London, taking the name of Israel ben Abraham. Lord Gordon became scrupulous in ritual observance, grew a long beard, and rebuked any Jew whom he perceived as nonobservant.

He was imprisoned for libel against the British government. While in jail, he conducted regular services, attempted to observe ka-

7

shrut, and ignored any Jew who did not have a beard. He died in prison but was not buried in a Jewish cemetery.

11. *Warder Cresson*

Cresson (1798–1860) was the earliest known United States proselyte. Though born into a Philadelphia Quaker family, Cresson was profoundly affected by his relationship with the early Reform Jewish leader, Isaac Leeser. In 1844, he decided to visit what is now Israel and, prior to his departure, was named honorary US consul to Jerusalem.

Though the title was withdrawn before he reached Jerusalem (certain US government officials considered Cresson a maniac), Cresson converted to Judaism in Jerusalem in 1848. Returning to Philadelphia to settle his affairs, he was declared insane by a court at the instigation of his wife and son. He appealed the case and won. He moved to Palestine in 1852 as Michael Boaz Israel, wrote extensively for the balance of his life, became a prominent member of the Sephardic community, and was buried on the Mount of Olives.

12. *Setsuzo Kotsuji*

A Japanese Hebraist, born in Kyoto, Japan, in 1899, of a family descended from a line of Shinto priests. As a youngster, he was converted to Christianity, attended the American Presbyterian College in Tokyo, and later came to the US to attend Christian seminaries.

Returning to Japan, he taught Old Testament and Hebrew at the theological seminary of Aoyama Gakuin University. Just before Japan's involvement in World War II, Kotsuji made strenuous efforts to help the Eastern European Jews who had found a haven in Kobe. In 1943, he wrote (in Japanese) a history of the Jewish people. In 1959, he went to Jerusalem to undergo formal conversion to Judaism and he took the name Abraham. Since that time, he has lectured to Jewish audiences in the US.

13. *Nahida Ruth Lazarus* (1849–1928)

A German playwright, novelist, and journalist who converted to Judaism after the death of her first husband. In 1895, she became the second wife of the philosopher, Moritz Lazarus. Her many novels and short stories have been forgotten, but she is remembered for her later writings on Jewish subjects.

14. *Aimé Pallière* (1875–1928)

French writer and theologian. He was born into a devout Catholic family. After a chance visit to the

9

Lyons Synagogue on Yom Kippur, he was drawn to Judaism and wanted to become a Jew. However, his advisor, the Italian liberal, Rabbi E. Benamozegh, convinced him to live as a Jew without full conversion to Judaism. He became a spiritual guide to the Paris Liberal Synagogue and the French Reform movement. For some time, he was president of the World Union of Jewish Youth.

15. Me
16. You

CHAPTER I

The Road to Judaism—
My Personal Story

DURING the years that I've been working with those who have chosen Judaism, I have come to see that Judaism is attractive to people of all faiths and backgrounds. I have met Jews who were originally Catholic and Jews who were originally Protestant, whether Baptists, Presbyterians, Episcopalians, or Christian Scientists. I have met Chicano Jews and Cajun Jews, Italian Jews and Black Jews. But, before you meet some of them, I want to tell you about my own personal road to Judaism.

I initially became aware of Judaism as a religion in high school, when I met Jews for the first time. I grew up as a Baptist, in an Italian family. I lived in a large city, in an Italian neighborhood. In elementary and junior high school most of my classmates came from the immediate area, so it wasn't until high school that Jews became a part of my peer group.

When I was a child, my family was active in the Baptist church, and I was a churchgoing, baptized Baptist. During my adolescent years, though, I underwent a crisis of faith.

11

Questions—about Jesus, about faith, about believing—
began to trouble me, and I found no answers. People just
kept telling me to pray harder or believe more or have
faith. I wanted answers, but nobody seemed able to give
them to me. I began to feel that my religion was meaning-
less and that I was going through empty motions. I began
to fall away from the church.

At that time I began reading about Judaism. My best
friend in high school was an observant Jew, and I was
attracted to what I perceived as a whole way of life. One
day, I impulsively told my mother that some day I was
going to convert to Judaism. She looked at me and said,
"Uh huh," used to my outrageous statements at that stage
of my life. Neither of us knew just how prophetic those
words would prove to be.

In college I took many courses in comparative religion
and Bible. I had always loved the Bible, having studied it
extensively as a Baptist. Yet the more I studied it, the
more drawn to Judaism I became. I was not yet ready to
talk about conversion, and, if anybody had asked me
what I was, I would have said, "Well, Protestant, I guess."
But I would have had to think about it. I was uncertain.

In retrospect I find it intriguing that I never considered
any religion other than Judaism. Though deeply dis-
satisfied with my own faith, I never undertook a system-
atic study of other religions, searching for options. The
Eastern religions held no attraction for me. As a matter of
fact, no religion held no real attraction for me—except
Judaism.

What I liked most about Judaism was that it was ori-
ented toward *this* life and *this* world in a very real way. It
seemed to give its followers a system to live by, a system

that at the same time had legal, spiritual, moral, and ethical components that were inseparable from the religion itself. Judaism never asked that things be accepted purely on faith. It gave each person an active role to play in the world as a genuine partner of God. Judaism emphasized living with my fellow people in *this* world, but also contained a deeply spiritual element which nourished and nurtured me. I was also drawn to Judaism because of its formidable and wonderful intellectual tradition, its sense of history and antiquity, its connection with an unbroken chain of people and traditions spanning almost 4,000 years! What a people! What a faith!

Many of my friends find it hard to believe that I really "chose" Judaism during high school. I had never attended a Jewish service, holiday celebration, or ritual of any kind. Indeed, I had no first hand experience with Judaism until college. Still, I knew. I liked my Jewish friends. I wanted to be like them and live like them. Judaism afforded them something special, though they didn't always realize it. They never tried to impress me, but I was impressed. Judaism was for me, and on some deep level I knew it was just a matter of time until I embraced this magnificent faith as my own.

Sometime during my college years, I really began to do Jewish things. I attended synagogue services for the first time. A Jewish friend of mine got married and I went to the wedding. I remember sitting in the synagogue feeling very strange. Even though I didn't participate in the ritual, even though the Hebrew was totally foreign to me, I felt an inexplicable bond to Judaism. The feeling persisted throughout my college years.

Immediately after college, I moved to New York City.

I dated a succession of Jewish men. More than one of them remarked that part of my attractiveness was that I was "so Jewish." They felt I was more "Jewish" than they were, and they loved it. I found that perception difficult to fathom, since the only "Jewish" thing I did at the time was read lots of Jewish books!

The truth is that I felt Jewish without really having lived Jewishly. I made the decision to become a Jew even though I really didn't know what lay ahead in terms of Jewish "doing." But then, most of the Jews I met at that stage of my life weren't doing anything Jewishly either. Becoming a Jew seemed very logical.

In my heart of hearts, I felt that I would become a Jew after college, but I spoke of it to no one. I kept reading books about Judaism and books about Jews. Most of my friends were Jews. Most of the men I dated were Jews. It became apparent to me that I could never marry anybody who wasn't Jewish. Then, as I was considering conversion, I met my husband-to-be. I finally decided to end my "fence sitting." This was serious. Even though I had already begun to consider myself "unofficially Jewish," the time had arrived for my formal conversion.

We talked about it, to be sure, but there was no debate. He was very relieved and said he would arrange for me to meet a rabbi. To this day, I don't know how he decided on the rabbi with whom I eventually studied, but I could not have made that phone call. I would have been terrified to call a rabbi and say I wanted to convert or to study. I had no idea how anybody converted to Judaism. I had never met anybody who had chosen to become Jewish. Despite extensive reading and study, I knew nothing about conversion! I felt stupid and helpless, as I sat there while my husband-to-be made the arrangements.

The next day I went by myself to meet "the rabbi." I had never met a rabbi before. It was the second time in my life I had set foot in a synagogue! Alone, I walked into the rabbi's study. From floor to ceiling there were books, big Jewish books! (He was a Conservative rabbi. My fiancé, Ben, had been reared as an Orthodox Jew but emphatically wanted an alternative to Orthodoxy.) So there I sat in this enormous office, all alone. I suddenly felt very small and very inadequate.

The rabbi entered and introduced himself. He then immediately tried to dissuade me from converting! He inundated me with questions! Had I really thought about conversion? Was I ready for it? How did I know this was what I wanted? I began to feel angry. After all, I had thought about conversion a great deal. I did want it, and it took a lot of courage for me to walk into that office. In spite of that, my motives were being challenged. *"You may be immature." "Your fiancé may be immature." "Your fiancé may be marrying you because he is rebelling against his own heritage."*

I had had enough! I let him know in no uncertain terms that I was going to convert, and if he was not interested in preparing me then I would find someone else with whom to study. But I was going to convert! That seemed to convince him. He said I could study with him individually over a period of time and when he thought I was ready I could convert. I was relieved and came to enjoy the course of study very much.

The rabbi demanded a great deal of me. I didn't develop a close personal relationship with him, because I always regarded him with awe. After all, he was my judge, the person who was going to pass or fail me! Though I learned a great deal, I wasn't attending services on a regular basis.

15

In fact, other than studying, I still wasn't doing anything Jewishly. So I was surprised when one day the rabbi said, "Okay now you're ready." I didn't feel ready. I thought he was just trying to finish up and get rid of me. Nevertheless, we set a time for my conversion ceremony.

The ceremony was a very private matter. It took place in the rabbi's office, and I felt like a passive participant in the process. I wasn't asked if I wanted anybody to attend the ceremony. The expectation was that the only people present would be me, my fiancé, and my future mother-in-law, and in fact that's who was there. What an emotional experience! I was both nervous and happy. In retrospect, however, I was also very angry that I didn't play a more active role in my own ceremony of conversion. I felt as if we were doing something behind closed doors, and I missed the opportunity to share with others my joy at becoming a Jew.

But enough of regrets! The actual ceremony was one of the most unforgettable moments of my life. Suddenly, despite the presence of others in the room, I stood alone, embracing a new self. I had a sense of undertaking something momentous when I was asked whether I would cast my lot with that of the Jewish people. At that instant, I made a life-altering decision. I affirmed that I was changing my destiny. I was joining my destiny with something transcendent, beyond myself. An unknown future beckoned, and that was frightening, yet thrilling.

It was remarkable. At that moment *I* cast my lot with that of the Jewish people. *I* was a Jew. I declared a willingness to bond myself to the Jewish people. I could hardly get the words out. I had tears in my eyes and I was shaking. I was a Jew.

I do want to mention my experience at the mikveh, the

16

ritual bath in which all male and female converts in Conservative and Orthodox Judaism immerse themselves prior to the ceremony itself. Though it is only now beginning to play a role in Reform Jewish life, I enthusiastically endorse its inclusion in the conversion process. The idea of the mikveh provoked tremendous anxiety within me. I had never seen one. Even though I had been told that I would immerse myself and say a blessing, it seemed very arcane. I was a wreck as we drove to the mikveh. Once I got there and became involved in the ritual, however, I loved it. I experienced a feeling of rebirth. I went in by myself. I immersed myself. I said blessings in Hebrew. I truly felt as though I were becoming a different person, a Jewish person. The experience did not feel like my Baptist baptism. It felt very different. I stumbled over the Hebrew blessings, but it didn't matter. The moment was highly charged, and decisively separated my non-Jewish and Jewish lives. I will never forget it.

Is the mikveh for everyone? Perhaps not. But I believe that such an option should be available in Reform Jewish life. I urge you to consider it as a personal option, and, should you find it an attractive possibility, discuss it with your rabbi.

When I woke up the morning after my conversion I felt wonderful. I felt sparkling new, excited, charged up. I wanted to start being Jewish. I said to my fiancé "What are we going to do now?" and he said, "What do you mean? What we're doing is just fine." What I hadn't realized until that moment was that I actually did not know where to begin or what to do. So long as I was involved in the academics of Judaism I knew what to do. I could study, I could read, I could learn. I could debate with myself or with my fiancé or with the rabbi. But, now, my course of study was over. Suddenly the rabbi was no longer available every week. I didn't have a weekly appointment set aside just for me. Now my Jewish future was in my hands. But what to do? I knew that the rabbi was a very busy person and I wasn't going to bother him. I didn't know any "doing" Jews at all except my future in-laws who lived in Brooklyn and who were in a sense still very foreign to me. I didn't feel comfortable asking them for help yet. In fact, I didn't know what to ask! I did not have a clue about where to begin. I was technically Jewish, and I wanted to "do" and feel Jewish—but I couldn't yet.

It never occurred to me that there would be an "after-the-conversion." I experienced a post-conversion depression. After all the excitement, I suddenly came to terms with the fact that I was Jewish but I didn't know how to practice Judaism. I didn't feel authentic performing rituals and I didn't know where to go for support. In a flash of insight, I understood what should have been clear all along. Conversion was not "the end" of anything! Instead, it marked a beginning! Again I was a beginner, albeit a little further along the road to Judaism. Suddenly I intuited that I had *always* been on a road toward Judaism. A long road still lay ahead of me which would ultimately lead to my feeling and being and doing Jewish, and feeling comfortable with it all.

This didn't discourage me. I was determined to do it, to learn and do more. Since that day, I have never ceased walking my personal road to increased Jewish literacy and commitment. That's why I am writing these words to you. I hope that you will also find much joy and fulfillment in Judaism, for the Jewish people needs *you!*

The Road to Judaism—Another Story

by Rachel

After several years of struggle and reading, five years of intermarriage, a few years of increasing Jewish religious practice, and a year and a half of concentrated study, I have made the decision to convert to Judaism. It is the interplay of thoughts, emotions, and experiences that have brought me to this decision. It has been a growth process. The overriding urge, the need at this time is to bring this process of growth to its completion. It is time to draw the disconnected pieces together and begin a life of wholeness.

My road to Judaism has been a complex one. Ironically, the complexity has given me the assurance all along that this was a genuine growth. The moment in which I felt ready for mikveh (a total readiness to immerse my whole being, to *become* Jewish) and ready to tell my parents of my decision was intense, and can only be compared to my decision to marry. It was a desire with all the resources of my being for commitment, yet it was accompanied by all the attendant doubts and fears of committing oneself to a future full of unknowns. It was a commitment based on faith.

When Arthur and I married I remember thinking that conversion to Judaism was not even in the realm of the possible. And even at the beginning of my year and a half of study I seriously doubted the possibility. Even though I was aware of not knowing much about Judaism, what

19

impresses me most now is how *little* I knew. This was due to my concept of conversion as a sudden radical change. I know it now to be a gradual process. Even though at this point I do not feel entirely Jewish, I find it almost inconceivable to imagine never celebrating Shabbat, never observing the holy days, never saying the Shema.

For years I had struggled with the theology of Catholicism, a theology which emphasizes *belief.* Once I seriously questioned that belief, the roots of my faith were shattered. Though I was taught that deeds were important, the stress was on having faith, on "believing in" something, even though or perhaps especially because it evaded all reason. In Judaism, by contrast, it is the emphasis on action, on righteous behavior that I find so attractive. The allowance, sometimes encouragement, of questions concerning belief, God, and truth is such a welcome relief. One *can* be religious and question; in fact, it is one's duty to question. Once I had learned that *Israel* meant "to struggle with God," I felt my destiny at hand.

For me, another attraction to Judaism is the principle of the sanctification of life. For years I have yearned for a life style in which religion is integral not peripheral. The concept of celebrating and loving all of life, and of making the ordinary holy, is supremely attractive: a constant devotion to God, which, rather than denying the earthly, the human, and the complex, celebrates them. Because I have found this possibility for the celebration and sanctification of life within Judaism through Shabbat, mitzvot, kashrut, tsedakah, the holidays, reading, study, and prayer, I wish to become a full member of Klal Yisrael, to pledge my life with that of the Jewish people.

My decision has not been an easy one. My strong Catholic upbringing, my attachment to the person of Jesus, my close family ties, as well as Arthur's ambivalence about Judaism before and during the first years of our marriage, served to delay any serious consideration of conversion until we made definite plans to start a family. We always knew we would have to resolve our conflict. Observing Catholicism became increasingly unsatisfying, not to mention my unhappiness in not being able to share the religious "me" with Arthur. It also became increasingly difficult for him to accompany me to Mass. Little by little, our mutual observance and knowledge of Judaism increased. Our providential meeting with a wonderful teacher at the time we planned to start a family and our subsequent study and friendship have blessed and enriched our lives immeasurably. The contacts and friends we have made since then indicate to us how much Judaism and being Jewish mean to us. It has become our way of life.

With a sense of obligation to continue a tradition, a tradition I have come to live, I choose to become Jewish. I pray that I am worthy of the task.

"All beginnings are difficult."

FROM THE MIDRASH

"Where people truly wish to go, there their feet will manage to take them."

FROM THE TALMUD

CHAPTER II

"But I Don't Feel Jewish!"

"I didn't feel Jewish or Christian. I was just sort of in between, sort of in a state of limbo. I wanted to be something, but I really didn't know how to go about doing it. I wanted to be Jewish, to lead that life, but I didn't know what to do."

JAN

DON'T expect to . . . yet. You didn't feel grown-up when you were born, either. You will eventually, but not through magic and not without effort. You have studied and gone through a conversion ceremony. This made you legally a Jew . . . but that is not the end. It's only the beginning of a lifelong process. There is a rich Jewish life to be led after the conversion ceremony, but you will have to take an active role in shaping that new reality. That's what this book is all about.

I had studied and was anxious for my conversion ceremony to take place. I wanted my Jewishness to be official, even though I didn't feel quite ready. But once it was official I remember how unprepared I felt. I was on my own, and it was scary. I didn't know if I was doing things the right way. I thought after my conversion I would know how to do everything perfectly, immediately. Instead, Judaism seemed a jumble, and I felt very insecure and defensive. Even when I did do something properly, I

23

didn't feel authentic. I didn't feel as though I *owned* Judaism. Judaism didn't feel *mine* yet, and I didn't know if it ever would. I was still closer to my non-Jewish past than my Jewish present. I suppose I expected a flash from the heavens to give me an instant personal *Jewish* past at the moment of my conversion. No such luck. It took practice and time, but it happened. And eventually you, too, will have a Jewish past to call your own.

> "I don't know if I totally feel Jewish yet. I don't know if I will ever get there. Even in the temple, when we go to services or to a meeting, I wonder if they know that I am a convert. I recently was thinking about asking the rabbi, the cantor, and the secretary, Does the Board of Directors know? Does the sisterhood know? I feel Jewish to a certain extent, but I can't compare it to anything because I wasn't born Jewish. I can only go by what I have inside."
>
> ALAN

There is no Jewish mystique. You don't have to be born a Jew to be a Jew and to feel and think Jewishly. You can *build* a Jewish identity, and the road to building identification and emotional commitment begins with learning. After a couple of months, you'll be surprised at your progress. Success breeds success, and before long you'll find yourself acquiring new knowledge and setting new and more ambitious personal goals as you create your new Jewish world.

In the Beginning

> "What I really needed was my own Jewish mother, but my mother-in-law was a little too threatened by my emerging Jewishness to help me as much as I needed. So I had to find

someone. In effect, I found a Jewish sister, a close and dear friend who became my personal one-woman Jewish university. I could call her with any question, at any time of the day or night—and I did!"

PAT

Find a Jewish model for yourself. It's easier and more fun to learn from somebody, by watching, asking, and doing—even if you feel awkward at first. There may be someone with whom you feel comfortable in your family-by-marriage. Or you may have a good friend who is Jewishly knowledgeable. If not, speak to a rabbi and ask about the possibility of an "adoptive" Jewish family.

When I became a Jew, my husband and I lived far away from our extended Jewish family. Fortunately, however, I found some friends who were quite Jewishly literate. We started a study group and met regularly to learn, to cook together for holidays, and just to be together. These friends gave me a great deal of support. I had a comfortable environment in which to learn and ask questions, while gradually becoming part of a Jewish community. By doing and learning I began to build my own Jewish past.

It is important to establish a Jewish environment in your home. If you don't already have Shabbat candlesticks, buy some. They should be lovely, but they don't have to be wildly expensive. Set them aside and use them only for Shabbat and holidays. Buy a mezuzah if you don't already have one. They are available in synagogue shops and stores which sell Jewish religious items. Read about the significance of the mezuzah and then have a mezuzah-affixing ceremony to dedicate your house or apartment as a Jewish home.

Buy a Jewish calendar. It's different from the secular Gregorian calendar that we use daily. It's a lunar calendar. The months have Hebrew names. Jewish days start at sundown of the previous Gregorian day. Look through the whole calendar and note all the Jewish holidays and when they occur.

Try to locate a bookstore that specializes in Jewish books and records, then go and browse. Jewish booksellers can be especially helpful resources once you get to know each other. They can recommend materials especially appropriate for you, so ask them for assistance and advice. For a basic suggested library of Jewish books and records, as well as a starter list of Jewish ritual objects you'll want in your home, see end of the book.

> "I spent a lot of time reading about Jewish holidays and rituals. There was so much, I didn't know where to begin, so I became paralyzed. I didn't do anything. But then, one day, I spent two hours memorizing the Shabbat blessing over the candles. I spent two hours the next day memorizing the blessing over the wine and two hours on the third day memorizing the blessing over the chalah. Then, on Friday night, *I* said them! That was the beginning. From then on, I knew I could do it!"
>
> HARVEY

Do! Start somewhere—anywhere. Don't set unrealistic goals for yourself. For instance, start a pattern of Shabbat observance. You will need to know the candle blessings and Kiddush. If you can read Hebrew, fine. If you can't read the Hebrew, don't worry. Practice saying the candle blessing several times until you can recite it with some facility. Then turn your energies toward the Kiddush. Use transliterations if need be to ease your way at first. Don't worry if you say the prayers slowly. Fluency will come. The most important thing is to start, and the second most important thing is to continue! Try to be consistent, and make the commitment to do it every week.

Records and tapes are an effortless way to learn. You can learn blessings, prayers, and songs from these, which often come complete with words, translations, and transliterations. In addition to records relating to Shabbat there are others that will teach you Jewish legends, songs for other holidays, and even how to conduct your own seder at Passover. Choose one, containing Shabbat blessings and songs, for example, and play it over and over as you do office work or household chores or as you prepare for Shabbat dinner. Not only will the songs establish a mood of anticipation of Shabbat, but you will learn them with surprising speed. After you master one record, proceed to another. In several months, you will have acquired quite a repertoire.

Read Jewish cookbooks. In addition to recipes, they will usually give you menus for holidays and Shabbat which you can use as a basis for experimentation and improvisation. Jewish cooking goes beyond chicken soup (although that's not a bad place to start and you certainly should know how to make it, if only for medicinal purposes!). Try your hand at kugel, kreplach, latkes, even gefilte fish (it's not as difficult as it's made out to be). These are all foods which the Jews of Eastern Europe brought with them to North America. The majority of Jews in the United States trace their origins to Eastern Europe, but Jews have lived in many lands, and Jewish cuisine reflects all of these varied cultures. You may, for example, want to familiarize yourself with the foods common to Sephardic (North African, Spanish, Portuguese, Greek, Syrian, Cuban, etc.) Jewish households. Dishes such as borekas and fritada may seem exotic to you at first, but they are just as authentically Jewish as matzah balls.

Visit synagogues in your area, and begin regular wor-

27

ship at one that feels comfortable to you. At first, none of them may seem "right." I felt that way. In the beginning, I was very uneasy at services and really didn't understand the Jewish mode of worship. I was not used to the prayers, and I was intimidated by the Hebrew. It seemed as though everyone knew Hebrew except me. Although I wanted to be at ease, I feared I never would be.

Don't be discouraged if you have these feelings. Buy the prayer book that the synagogue uses and look it over. Practice your Hebrew reading at home. You will feel more comfortable with the Hebrew in time. The synagogue can be an important resource because it offers you a community, a support system. There may be chavurot (social and/or learning groups) which you can join for informal learning and celebration of holidays. Most synagogues have adult education classes where you can study and experience a wide variety of Jewish subjects including Israeli dancing, Bible, Hebrew, cooking, Jewish ethics, theology, and synagogue skills.

The important thing is to start somewhere. As you grow more secure in your Jewishness, you can add to your Jewish "repertoire." Don't be impatient. You won't get it all right away. Nobody does. The process is not easy or instantaneous, but it is fun and it is rewarding. Your steady progress will help you to move forward and to develop a Jewish momentum. What you are learning and doing will slowly become internalized. You will make Judaism your own, and you will feel authentic.

If you are single, it is even more important to join a temple, to create your own community. You will need the support of other Jews. As importantly, you will want to have others—perhaps other Jewish singles—with whom to share your Jewish growth. It has often been noted that

Judaism is a family-oriented religion. In recent years, however, Jewish institutions have become more and more responsive to the special needs of those Jews who are single. In addition to the Jewish singles family that you may build, you should also have a Jewish "host" family with whom to share Jewish holidays and other experiences. Your rabbi will be happy to make this connection for you.

But there are other feelings that may accompany your first days or months as a Jew. It is natural to feel ambivalence and/or loss. You may grieve over the separation from your own past. You may feel that "you can never go home again," that you've given up what was familiar for a strange, confusing new world. It may seem as though you'll never be accepted or acceptable.

The transforming moment in my conversion ceremony occurred when the rabbi asked me if I willingly cast my lot with that of the Jewish people. At that moment, I saw both of my worlds—one, familiar but receding, and one, largely unknown, toward which I was turning. I felt awed, sad, happy, lost, and found all at once. All those feelings are natural and normal. You are doing something that most people never do. You are consciously making a fundamental change in your life. Try to confront these feelings of ambivalence and loss without feeling guilty about them. As your security in your new identity grows, you will feel them less and less. You *can* go home again, but on different terms, as we'll discuss in Chapter III.

I discovered that, despite my sensations of loss and insecurity, I developed a strong conviction that I'd chosen the right path. Beyond my misgivings, I knew that Judaism offered me a system for living that I could embrace and a system of values in which I could feel great pride.

29

From Others Who Have Been There

"I expected myself to be more than other people expected. I expected more of myself than anyone expected of me."

DAN

"It's nice to live in a Jewish way. It's nice to be able to show people how you feel through your actions."

CINDY

"When I became Jewish and went through my conversion ceremony, I didn't feel very Jewish. Today, I'm beginning to feel Jewish because I can light the Shabbat candles all by myself, say the prayers by myself, and feel a very warm feeling. I feel the love."

MAUREEN

"Memory is the diary we all carry about with us."

ANONYMOUS

"Honor thy father and thy mother"

TORAH

CHAPTER III

Your Non-Jewish Family

SOME PEOPLE—at least in the beginning—choose not to tell their parents about their conversion. They decide that it would be too difficult a situation for their parents—and for them—to deal with. I know of one woman, in fact, who has been a Jew for over twenty years and who has never told her mother and father for fear of hurting them.

You know your parents best, certainly better than I do, and ultimately you will have to decide when and how to inform them of your Jewishness. Waiting may allow you a bit more "space" in your Jewish beginnings. As your family realizes that you have begun to celebrate Jewish holidays and participate in Jewish life, questions are bound to arise that may provide an opportunity for you and them to talk.

How do you tell them? The direct approach, while you may dread it and it may be painful for everyone at the time, has the advantage of defining your position at once. Your parents will know that you are a Jew now. You can not legitimately be expected to observe Christian holidays. Above all, you can begin to build your relationship on a set of new, and hopefully shared, assumptions.

The indirect approach gives you time and a measure of

family calm. You can gradually acclimate your parents and family to your Jewishness. On the other hand, since your parents have never been officially told that you are Jewish, the potential for hurtful misunderstanding is far greater than it would be with a direct "announcement."

If you choose the direct approach, it is best to tell your parents in person. Go to them. Pick a time that will be quiet and free of distractions. They may react positively, and, if they do, that's terrific! However, be prepared for them to be surprised and upset. They may express bitterness and hurt. They may feel that you are rejecting them personally. They may feel that they have somehow failed.

Remain calm. Reassure them of your love for them. Reassure them that you are still their child, that they will always be a part of you and you of them, that nothing can ever change that. Remember that this will not be the only time that you and your parents will need a sense of mutual support in word or deed. As difficult as that moment may be, keep in mind the numerous opportunities you will have over the years to show your parents that they have not lost you, that you are and always will be with them.

In a very few instances, parents are never able to accept their child's conversion. These parents are usually fundamentalist Christians, who sincerely feel that conversion to Judaism condemns their son or daughter to eternal damnation. Should this be your experience, I can only urge you not to be too discouraged. Embrace your Jewish family and community even more closely. Hopefully, in time, your parents will come to realize that their love for you should and must transcend their feelings about your decision.

33

"I called my mother on the phone to tell her that I was converting to Judaism. When I finished, there was a long silence at the
other end of the line. Then she said simply, 'Why are you
converting? Why can't he convert instead?' "

CINDY

You may have received a less than enthusiastic response from your family when they learned that you were
converting to Judaism. Don't be surprised, and, above all,
don't be hurt or disappointed. Although it is nice to have
approval, don't expect it. Your family might not be able
to give you approval at first. They are in a difficult situation, and it is just as important to understand their feelings as it is to understand your own.

Your parents have a great deal invested in you—many
years, great sacrifice, dreams and plans for your future. If
they are religiously committed, they undoubtedly saw to
it that you received a good religious education in addition
to public or private school. Accordingly, they may experience your decision to convert as a rejection of them or of
their way of life.

They may wonder how you can be their child and yet
choose to be so different from them. They may fear that
they have lost you, so it is especially important to show
them that they haven't. You must emphasize that, even
though you have made a different choice, your love and
respect for them will always be unchanged. You are now
a part of two families, and a bridge between them as
well.

"My son was about to observe his bar mitzvah, and I remember
calling my parents and inviting them out for lunch. We met in
a restaurant and had a lovely time for about an hour. Finally I
said, 'I came here to talk to you about something important.'

What had been a very lovely luncheon suddenly became a very tense encounter. I told them that Paul was about to become a bar mitzvah, and that it was very important to me and to him to have his grandparents participate in the ceremony. I knew it was awkward for them, but I wanted them to participate on a level that was comfortable for them. My mother began to cry. She hadn't attended our wedding, and I guess the thought of a big family celebration after all these years was a little overwhelming for her. But I showed her and Dad some of the readings we had chosen and I told them about the service. I also showed them the parts that I had in mind for them. It worked beautifully. Everyone was involved. And I think that the bar mitzvah experience finally settled everything down. Our family is more of a family than we ever were."

SUSAN

Your family should always feel connected to you, even though they may be unfamiliar with your new observances and customs. In the beginning, you might all be uncomfortable. It may be best not to invite them for Jewish holidays at first. If they do happen to be with you, explain what you're doing, but be careful that you don't sound preachy or heavy handed, lest you make your family even more defensive.

"After I converted to Judaism, the strangest thing happened. My mother sent a birthday card to my brother but forgot my birthday . . . which was strange, because we're twins!"

TERRY

Neither you nor your parents should ever think of your conversion to Judaism in terms of one side winning and one side losing. If that happens, everyone is the loser. You are still their child and you will always be a part of their family. You should express that to them. You will always be there to help them celebrate holidays, but some things

35

will be different. Although you are the same person, by your conversion to Judaism you have committed yourself to some profound changes. You will have to teach your family that you have a Jewish identity. This will not be easy at first, and it will not happen overnight for at least two reasons.

First, you probably have not yet completely established a solid Jewish identity for yourself, much less for anyone else. You may not "feel" Jewish at this point, but you will have to begin to present yourself as Jewish to others. Start slowly. Begin by quietly remembering that you are now a Jew. As your family realizes that you observe Jewish holidays and customs, your identity as a Jew will begin to assert itself. You need merely concentrate on Jewish doing. In that way you will avoid excessive discussion and let your actions speak for you. In the process of doing, you will begin to "feel" more Jewish, making it easier for you to project a Jewish identity.

The second reason that your family will not see you as a Jew immediately is very simple. They have known you your entire life. It is difficult enough for parents to see their children as adults, much less as adults who have made such a major change. You may be uncomfortable with your new identity in the beginning. You may feel like familiar strangers. You will all need time. You might even need space. It is very difficult for some people to be with their families at all in the days immediately following conversion. You might find it easier to be on your own while you settle into your Jewish self. If you feel that you do need to separate yourself emotionally and physically from them for a while, don't feel guilty. This will not be permanent. You will find your own way of being part of your family on your own terms.

"In the middle of my son's bar mitzvah service, we were marching around with the Torahs and my whole family was sitting together. As we marched around, my uncle took my arm, pulled me aside to him, looked at me with tears in his eyes and said, 'I am so proud of you.' And I was delighted and stunned and amazed because it was the first time that I really felt that he accepted me on my own terms. That bar mitzvah really marked my own rite of passage and coming of age."

LOIS

It all takes time, but remember that the change in your family's perception of you will not come with time alone. You will have to work at it. First, you will have to establish your Jewish identity for yourself. Secondly, you must establish it repeatedly, in ways large and small, for your parents. Don't be impatient with them or with yourself.

My parents were initially apprehensive and hurt by my intention to become Jewish. They felt that my fiancé should have been asked to convert to Christianity. They saw it as their side losing and another side winning. I explained to them that conversion was not, as I have mentioned, a favor, something one does *for* someone else. I had considered conversion to Judaism long before my fiancé and I ever discussed it. He did not ask me to convert. Instead, we talked about our respective religions, and, when the discussion got around to the kind of home we wanted to establish, it became clear that we wanted it to be a Jewish home.

Although I was very satisfied with my decision to choose Judaism, my parents' perspective was that I was leaving the religion of my family and embracing an alien faith. They felt that, in the process, I was also abandoning them. They were hurt, even though I was aware of their feelings and tried to be as sensitive as possible. Yet those

37

initial feelings did not last forever. They were very fond of my husband and that made it easier. I also made it clear to them that I was still a part of the family and that would never change. And it hasn't.

But my parents also had to understand that, although I could be with them and help them celebrate their holidays, I would no longer celebrate them as *my* holidays.

"The first Christmas after my conversion, my husband and I arrived at my parents' house early on Christmas morning. I knew that everyone would be anxious, and that impression was confirmed as soon as we walked in the house. My parents greeted us at the door, ushered us into the living room, sat us down around the Christmas tree, and promptly burst into tears. My husband was embarrassed and I wished I had never dragged him into this."

CAROL

It was difficult at first for my mother to be in my house in December and see no Christmas decorations or Christmas tree. Over the years, however, she has gotten used to it and has come to accept it.

My family frequently sends greeting cards. On our wedding day, my mother gave us a very nice card expressing her wishes that God would bless us on our wedding day. This was a fine sentiment, but there on the front of the card was a large gold cross! I was irritated, my husband bemused. Her sentiments and motivation were sincere, and I honestly don't think she thought the cross would bother us. She sent us cards for all occasions, but now she sends them only on Jewish occasions, such as Passover, Rosh Hashanah, and Chanukah.

She has managed very well with a difficult situation, and I admire her greatly. It is more important to her that we be together as a family than which holidays we do or do not celebrate. And she is happy that our children are being brought up with a religion, even if it is not hers. They are her grandchildren and she loves them and is proud of them. And they love her as well!

My entire family came out for my son's bar mitzvah. They had never been to my house before and, after I invited them, I wondered what I had done. I dreaded their coming as much as I was looking forward to it. As the bar mitzvah approached, the dread grew because I didn't really know what to expect. They came and spent a week with us. This visit was special because they saw my Jewish house, a house with Jewish books and a mezuzah on the door. They shared a Shabbat with us and our son's becoming a bar mitzvah with us and they loved it. They even helped cook! I was thrilled to see how excited they were. They said they had been to other ceremonies, but they had never seen a "real bar mitzvah," as they put it. They are anxiously making plans two years from now to come for my daughter's bat mitzvah. I am overjoyed.

We all have come a long way—together. With the passage of time, we have grown to accept and respect each other's differences and discovered that those differences do not divide us.

From Others Who Have Been There

"We celebrate Christmas with our family. We have dinner and exchange gifts. Of course, all our relatives know that we are Jewish, so they put little name tags on our packages. My aunts are especially careful to give us non-Christmas cards. One of my favorite aunts is a Christian, and, when Henry Winkler came up in discussion, she turned to me and said, 'Henry Winkler, isn't he of your faith?' "

LOUISE

"The first year after I converted to Judaism, we didn't go to my parents' house for Easter. When I told my mother that we couldn't come, she was very upset because she had already bought all the food. But now she knows that Easter comes during Passover."

PETER

"I gave up trying to communicate with my mother and father. I knew that they would never accept my conversion. I thought it might be easier to communicate with my siblings, so my husband and I made a special trip to see them and tried to get to know one another better. We spent a marvelous weekend together, and I was thrilled. Needless to say, it was a bitter disappointment when, four days later, we received a packet of 'salvation' materials in the mail from them, expressing the hope that we might see the light and be saved."

THERESA

"At this point, I don't think that my conversion is as well accepted as I would like it to be. We just sweep it under the carpet, and nothing is said about it. My family feels the less they know, the better it is. And I guess that's the way it has to be."

KEVIN

"I insisted on having a Jewish wedding, and I knew that my father felt extremely uncomfortable. He wasn't offended, but he has a lot of pride. I think he felt a little foolish preparing for a wedding in a religious tradition he knew nothing about. He was afraid he would look foolish in front of his friends. But he went through with it, and, afterwards, he was thrilled that we had had this kind of wedding. His friends accepted it as a warm family event. Everyone walked down the aisle. It was the first

40

time that our Protestant friends went to a Jewish wedding, and they loved it. I think the fact that his friends accepted it made it okay for him.''

M A R G A R E T

A Letter to My Non-Jewish Parents

Dear Mom and Dad,

I know how surprised you were when I told you of my decision to convert to Judaism. I am writing this letter to you because I am not sure how much our conversation resolved in your own minds. I want you to know that I love you both very much. You are my parents and I'm proud of the way you are. You have loved me all my life, have been there for me when I've needed you, and have given me everything I have ever needed, whether it was an advance in my allowance or a shoulder to cry on. You have shown patience, insight, and concern. And you have been my teachers. You have encouraged me to be everything I could be, and have provided me with every opportunity. You have helped to make me who I am. For all this and more that can never be spoken or written, I love you.

Now I come to you to tell you about a path which I have chosen and to ask for your support again. The choice I have made is very important and one which I believe will enrich my life.

Being a religious person is central to my life. You taught me that through your example. I will always treasure my childhood memories. Nothing can or ever will change that, for those memories are too precious to me. The path

I am on still confuses me because it is a little unfamiliar. But it is a way that I have chosen after much study and soul searching. It is not a path that leads me away from you. Please know that. You must never see it as such. Even though I have made a different choice, I will always be me, your child. We have so much to share! Now I ask for your understanding and love. I know that this may be difficult for you to accept right now, but I know that there is enough love among us. Our love will take us a long way. I also know that we can communicate and understand one another, just as we have always done, because we are a very special family. May God bless you both.

> Your loving daughter,
> *Amy*

A Letter to My Non-Jewish Family

Dear Family:

As you may have surmised, Susan and I have nurtured an interest in Judaism since our marriage. We had initially doubted that we could ever adopt the tradition as our own in any meaningful way. Those were the sentiments expressed in the letter to you announcing our engagement. Since that time though, our judgment changed and we decided to affiliate ourselves through conversion with a Reform congregation. We sing weekly in a small choir during services on Friday evenings and have both taken introductory Hebrew lessons. We have also, fortunately, made several friends and are feeling increasingly comfort-able as time passes.

Our decision was not a hasty one, nor was it one which received significant encouragement from friends or foes of any persuasion. It was of our own choosing and was predicated by both our needs to act responsibly and con-cretely in demonstrating and proclaiming our religious selves. We were thinking as well of the importance of offering to our children a tradition of religious practice and faith with which we both feel comfortable. Such would not have been possible for either of us had we remained in the fold of Christianity. Our decision was at its roots made in "fear and trembling" but with hope and not a small amount of courage. We trust that you can see it as such, and respect and accept our effort at approx-imating truth as we discern it, in worshiping the one God as we perceive Him.

The question of holidays is a difficult one which will be addressed throughout the remainder of our lives. It is not an enviable task to be a person of religious concerns in our society—much less one of a minority religion. Thus, in the future when we decline wholehearted participation in Christmas or Easter celebrations in favor of more ecumen-ical holidays like Thanksgiving and birthdays, it is not a rejection of you but rather an affirmation of our own religious yearnings as observant Jews. It is one of the ways in which we choose to reaffirm to ourselves and others symbolically that we are different in significant, un-ashamed ways. Such actions are certainly not requisite for one claiming to be Jewish. Indeed, some Jewish homes do contain Christmas trees and Easter eggs—though sadly so, in our view. I would anticipate that with the passage of years and the mutual gaining of confidence in our intentions that religious holiday sharing, whether Passover and Chanukah or Easter and Christmas, will not seem as awkward a possibility. Such will come, though I am sure not without some tears and anxiety on all our parts. It is your choice as much as ours.

If you are distressed with questions or even feelings of failure, that would seem understandable. And we affirm to you our sanity and good behavior and your own continuing worth to us. Hopefully, we can avoid theological disputation since our differences in that realm should be obvious. Moreover, if religion were only a matter of rational theological discourse, differences among Christians, Moslems, and Jews would have been settled long ago. At best, we can offer you only the opportunity to share with us in some way the tribulations of heart and mind which we will encounter in coming years. We cannot force you to accept such a gift nor can we apologize for the unsolicited challenge which our nonconformity presents to your own life choices. Regardless of the source, such challenges, whether elicited from the inchoate perturbations of a young mind or the incisive cynicisms of a gray-haired savant, can render any life more pregnant with possibility, more laden with mystery, indeed more thunderstruck with meaning. Differences among humankind, even between parent and child, while easily breeding despair, should also engender hope. It is our prayer that this "uncommon bang" of difference will do just that.

At a clergy institute during the spring, which was aimed at fostering understanding between Christian and Jew, a benediction was spoken embodying a spirit of dialogue which Susan and I also intend with this letter. It included the following words:

With malice toward none, with charity for all, with firmness in the right, as God gives us to see the right.

. . . So spoke Lincoln in 1865, so spoke our rabbi last spring, so speak the two of us today. And, finally, the ancient priestly benediction, a prayer from our childhoods first heard on the lips of generally sincere and gentle Baptist preachers, first understood in the haunting Hebraic voice of an uncommonly poetic, truly wise rabbi:

The Lord bless you and keep you.

The Lord look kindly upon you and be gracious to you.

The Lord bestow His favor upon you and give you peace.

With gratitude for the life and love which you have given us, we remain devotedly husband and wife, your children.

Shalom,
Eric/Susan

CHAPTER IV

Your Jewish Family

"I remember the first time I went to synagogue with my husband's family. We went in two cars, and his parents got there a few minutes before we did. I walked into the temple and found my mother-in-law informing all of her friends 'My Jewish daughter-in-law, who used to be a Baptist, is coming.' "

BONNIE

IN ADDITION to becoming part of the Jewish people, you, by marrying a born-Jew, have become part of a Jewish family. They may embrace you with open arms and you may indeed feel welcome. If you have been blessed with such a family, you don't need to read further. But, more often than not, both you and your Jewish family may face some very real difficulties with communication and expectations.

I think that most families sincerely want to provide a caring atmosphere for a new daughter- or son-in-law. But often they may be just as unsure and nervous as you are. The best of intentions can sometimes be misread and misinterpreted as condescension, insensitivity, or even hostility.

46

"My father-in-law said that it wasn't the religious issue he objected to in our marriage. It was my rotten personality!"

TONY

"My husband and I had very little money when we were first married. So when we went to visit my in-laws and the airline gave me some sandwiches, I brought them home with us. One of them was a ham sandwich. It never occurred to me that I shouldn't have brought it home. Maybe I should have known. But I was pregnant, I was sick, and I was tired. Anyway, my mother-in-law opened the refrigerator later. She took one look at the sandwich and started screaming at me. She told me that now she would have to throw away the refrigerator, and that it was my fault!"

MICHELLE

All Jewish families are not the same. Some know more about Judaism, some less. Some may feel more positively about their Jewishness, some less, and those factors may be very important to your interaction. If members of your Jewish family are very knowledgeable about Judaism and positive about their Jewishness, they may seem intimidating to you. They may be afraid of intimidating you. In their concern not to seem too demanding or imposing, they may not give you clear or consistent signals. They may ask nothing, Jewishly, of you, thus possibly conveying the implicit message "They think I can't do it" or "They don't want me to do it," or "They don't care," when, in fact, they may be hesitant to expect too much too soon.

"In the early years, I remember holidays with my Jewish family. Whenever it was my turn to participate, they would say: 'Oh give her something in English.' I was not permitted to participate in anything that was truly sacred. It really bothered me."

ZINA

47

An honest attempt to avoid alienating you, then, could be totally misconstrued.

On the other hand, your Jewish family may try too hard. I have a friend whose first Chanukah was spent with her Jewish family. With the entire household gathered around the table, they painstakingly explained every aspect of Chanukah to her. Under other circumstances, she would have been happy to have the information. In this setting, however, although their motives were admirable, her Jewish family only succeeded in making her feel self-conscious, distant, different—and angry.

Whatever the difficulties of the first tentative attempts at communication, if you have a knowledgeable and positive family, you have, potentially, a great resource. You can learn a lot from them, informally, as you celebrate holidays and Shabbat.

> "We were sitting around the dinner table and I told my cousins by marriage that I always light candles on Friday night. They turned to their wives and said, 'It would be nice if you would do that!' The women were embarrassed and said, 'Well, my mother used to do that.'"
>
> ELAINE

On the other hand, if members of your Jewish family are not very knowledgeable and/or feel ambivalent about their Jewishness, you might find yourself in a peculiar situation. Jewish learning does not come automatically at birth. Some born-Jews received an inadequate religious education during their childhood, and do not pursue Jewish learning during their adult years. They may identify strongly as Jews and "feel" very Jewish without knowing a great deal about ritual and holiday observance, Jewish

48

philosophy, theology and other basic teachings. You, however, came to Judaism and learned about it as an adult. As a result, you may know many things that members of your Jewish family do not. This can be very threatening to them because it makes them feel inadequate. In addition, if members of your Jewish family are ambivalent or negative about their own Jewishness, they may find it difficult to understand your choice altogether. They may feel threatened or hostile in encountering one who has *chosen* to become Jewish and who has positive feelings about it.

Do not let the negative or ambivalent feelings of others, even if they are family members, influence you. You can understand why they feel that way, but you will also have to understand that they cannot be a resource for you. You will have to look elsewhere for your role models. A friend who was new to Judaism told me of the difficulties she was having with her mother-in-law, who was not Jewishly knowledgeable. When confronted with the questions of her daughter-in-law, who was eager to learn and observe, she became short-tempered and defensive. If that happens, go elsewhere for your answers. In time, perhaps your Jewish family will learn from you.

"It was the first night of Chanukah and we went to Mel's parents' house to celebrate. Mel's father did the first two blessings. I knew that you're supposed to do three blessings on the first night because the Shehecheyanu is sung on the first night in addition to the other two. Everyone kind of looked at me. I felt as if I was in the wrong religion. But I really kept pressing it, because I knew that there was another blessing. Finally, my father-in-law said, 'You're right, there is another one.' I felt relieved. And the nicest thing was that I knew the blessing and

49

so I was able to do it! It was a very special moment in my life as a Jew.''

PAULA

"I guess the happiest moment of my Jewish life came to me when my mother-in-law appeared at our door and asked to speak to me privately. With tears in her eyes she said to me, 'I want to be a mother to you, but I don't know how. Will you help me?' ''

FRAN

In summary, then, you may find the clear direction you need from your Jewish family. If you don't, at least know that it might be because they *can't* give it to you, and not because they don't *want* to. The more you know, the more secure in your Jewish identity you'll become. You will feel comfortable within the family in time. The newness of the situation will wear off and you will have come to know and trust each other more.

Remember that you will have to allow time for your new in-laws to know you as a Jew. Even though you have already chosen Judaism and have become a Jew, your Jewish family will still need some months, perhaps years, to adjust to your new status. Be patient.

The ideal relationship will be a reciprocal one. Because they were born Jewish, your in-laws can be a resource for you, filling in gaps in your Jewish "past" and sharing their Jewish past with you. In a very real sense, they can become your teachers.

You, in turn, because you were not born Jewish, can also become their teacher. You can teach them to see Judaism through new eyes—your eyes. You will all be enriched by the experience of mutually teaching and learning about Judaism, its beauty and its meaning.

50

Of course if you are married, a great deal of your relationship with your Jewish family will depend on your relationship with a specific member of that family—your spouse. . . .

From Others Who Have Been There

"Let me tell you about the chicken soup. When I finally got to the point when I thought I had mastered chicken soup pretty well, I made it for my husband. He's my most valuable critic. He tasted it and said, 'This is good soup!' But he also told me that it wasn't like his mother's chicken soup. That's the funny part. His mother gave me the recipe!"

LESLIE

"Bill's family didn't really accept me. They didn't like the idea that I was a convert. The only one who really took me under her wing was his grandmother. She accepted me. She loved me. As a matter of fact, the last thing that she ever said to me was 'Have a baby.' She wanted a future for us. She was very loving and she kept explaining Yiddish to me. She became my mentor. And to this day I always try to remember: 'How did grandma light the candles, and what words did grandma use?' I felt very close to her. She was really my Jewish role model."

GEORGINA

"I really wanted to have my own seder. I studied all year, and finally felt that I was ready. There was only one problem. Carl's family was too far away to come to our seder, and I certainly couldn't invite my family. But I had an idea. I called up one of the local Jewish organizations and arranged to invite a new Russian immigrant family to our house for Passover. They had never been to a seder before. So there we were, two Jewish

51

families; one whose members were born Jewish but who knew nothing about how to run a Passover seder, and my Jewish family with me, a new Jew, conducting the seder. It was fabulous. Everything went just as I dreamed that it would. I can't imagine ever having a nicer seder. I loved it!''

BETH

"When a soul is sent down from heaven, it contains both male and female characteristics. The male elements enter the boy baby, the female, the girl baby; and, if they be worthy, God reunites them in marriage."

FROM THE *ZOHAR,*
a book of Jewish mysticism

CHAPTER V

Your Jewish Spouse

"God creates new worlds constantly by causing marriages to take place."

from the *Zohar*

THIS TEACHING from the Jewish mystical tradition is nowhere more true than in a marriage between a Jew by birth and a Jew by choice. For in truth, the home that emerges from that union is a new world, a synthesis of two biographies, two families and two religious traditions suddenly brought together under a single roof.

New worlds inevitably bring new challenges. It is therefore likely that your relationship with your spouse will be the single greatest factor in determining Judaism's impact on your life and the life of your family. In the best of circumstances, a Jewish spouse can be a teacher, a support, and a spiritual guide. All too often, however, and for the most complex of reasons, the Jewish spouse can also become a stumbling block and an active opponent of your Jewish development, hindering that development, and engendering feelings of frustration, ambivalence, and self-doubt. Let's consider a few of the things that you should know and recognize as post-conversion realities. Then we will consider how to deal with them, and, I hope, turn them to advantage.

> "My whole life, my parents had constantly told me how opposed they would be if I married someone who wasn't Jewish. When I started dating Kathy, I didn't have a moment's peace. There were phone calls and letters and tears and tantrums. But what a difference once Kathy decided to become a Jew. All of a sudden, we were welcomed in my parents' home. The tension evaporated. It was quite a relief."
>
> FRANK

1. *Conversion to Judaism will usually alleviate resistance to your marriage in your Jewish family.* That's a plus, for it means that your spouse's relationship with his or her parents will probably be free of the sort of tension that may characterize the current state of your relationship with your mother and father. One less conflict. One less concern. But please do not misunderstand me. Lessening tension in your Jewish spouse's family is no reason for conversion. Becoming a Jew is not a favor that one person does for another. If you have made a personal decision to become a Jew, fine. If you feel good about it, and are ready to embrace Judaism, that's wonderful. But conversion to Judaism as a response to a demand will ultimately lead to trouble and to heartbreak. The match between a new Jewish soul and the Jewish people must be a willing one on both sides.

> "I had just rattled off a list of all of the things that I wanted to change in our home: ritual observance, service attendance, and dietary restrictions. When I said that I wanted to keep a kosher home, my husband looked at me in horror. A flash of recogni-

55

tion crossed his eyes, and he yelled aloud, 'Oh, my god. I married my mother!' "

PATSY

2. *Once you have converted to Judaism, you are no longer the same person to whom your spouse was initially attracted.* As a Jewish new-born, you are not "my non-Jewish fiancé" any more. All of us know couples who attribute any and all problems in their relationship to the fact that "he/she changed," whether that is truly the root cause or not. But conversion *is* a change, a *real* change, and should be recognized as such.

"My husband never negates anything I do Jewishly. He lets me do whatever I want. I have taken over, and he doesn't resist. So we do things my way. That's all."

GAY

3. *As one who has chosen Judaism as an adult, you will probably be far more committed to Jewish study and to observance of the ritual aspects of Judaism than your spouse.* This is normal and natural. Judaism is new to you. It's fresh. It's exciting. It is life transforming. But don't expect your spouse to feel the same way, at least at first. By this stage in life, your husband or wife carries a great deal of baggage, Jewishly speaking. He or she is already the product of a Jewish upbringing, and may embrace a Jewish identity that is ethnically, rather than ritually, based. Personal observances, ambivalences, and even hostilities have already fallen into a certain pattern of feeling and doing. Don't expect your spouse to change overnight. Change is difficult under any circumstances. Allow your spouse the same respect that you would desire for yourself under similar circumstances.

"I made a mistake once that I will never make again. We were at my in-laws' house, and there was a discussion about Judaism going on. David's mother said something that was incorrect about the history of Judaism. I knew the right answer, and was so excited that I knew it that I corrected her in front of David and David's father. Talk about looks that can kill! From now on, I'll let David correct his mother."

ABBY

4. *Remember that you may know more about Judaism than your spouse or his/her family.* Don't be obnoxious about it. You will only cause yourself unnecessary pain. The ideal solution in this instance is to grow together, which we will discuss a little later in this chapter.

My personal experience reflected each of these four major challenges. I'd like to share that story with you, as well as the solutions that my husband and I developed together. They worked for us, and hopefully they will work for you as well.

Conversion was never an issue in my relationship with my husband. For a number of years I had been very interested in Judaism, had studied it, and knew I wanted to become Jewish. Once we decided to get married, *I* announced my intention to become a Jew. The real problems began *after* the conversion ceremony. Almost twenty years later, I can laugh at the irony of the situation. Then, however, it was deadly serious.

My spouse was comfortable with his Jewishness. It was something he took for granted, a part of him, like blue eyes or curly hair. He had grown up in a very observant home, in a totally Jewish neighborhood.

I, on the other hand, was new at this and was taking nothing for granted. In addition, I was excited! I was

57

learning, questioning, anxious to do. And I was determined.

We were on a collision course. My husband was satisfied with the way we were at that point—seder with his family, High Holy Days, and "knowing" we were Jewish. I, on the other hand, felt that I had *chosen* something, and I wanted more than that. So, in shocked disbelief, my husband watched the person he married slowly turning into a religious zealot! He envisioned himself being dragged back into his Jewish past, against his will, and he didn't like that one bit! He was vehement in his protests.

I wanted him to be enthusiastic and to have the same Jewish drive I had, and I was disappointed and angry at his resistance. (And somewhere too, I must confess, I was concerned lest I really *become* a zealot.) No Jewish demands were made of me. While that wasn't entirely bad, it gave me no standard for self-assessment. This was frustrating. I wanted a "grade," but it seemed as if my husband had *no* Jewish expectations of me. Whatever I did or didn't do was fine. It was maddening.

Only later did I come to realize that my husband did not give me Jewish cues for two reasons:

a. He didn't want to put undue pressure on me.

b. He was not ready himself to give cues. Though he had a rich Jewish education and a deep sense of his own Jewishness, he was in a period of Jewish inactivity and transition. Our Jewish life together, then, had to be created and achieved by our joint efforts.

We learned to talk to one another, to try to express our concerns, expectations, and fears. We decided to make Jewishness a pleasure rather than a burden. Our

Jewish observance would be determined by what we were *both* ready to do, *positively,* at a given time. In this way, creating our Jewish home and life style became a process, something in which we were jointly involved as partners.

Just for the record, here are a few of the major decisions we reached together, in the approximate order in which we originally made them:

1. Putting a mezuzah on our door.
2. Lighting Shabbat candles, chanting the Kiddush, reciting the Motzi, and having Shabbat dinner each week.
3. Making a firm decision that we would not go out on Friday night except to friends' homes for Shabbat or to Shabbat services.
4. Having our own Passover seder.
5. Committing ourselves to regular weekly study with a group of friends.
6. Building a sukah in our yard and buying a lulav and etrog.
7. Enrolling our daughter in a Jewish nursery school.
8. Changing our kitchen to a kosher kitchen.
9. Sending our daughter to a Jewish day school.
10. Extending Shabbat from Friday night into Saturday, including regular attendance at services as a family, and spending the entire afternoon of Shabbat together.

Our "committee of two" adopted each of these decisions unanimously. Early in our marriage, not one of them could have been adopted positively and enthusiastically. But with time, good communication, and mutual sensitivity, we were able to shape our Jewish life style the way we *both* wanted it to be.

Some Suggestions for You and Your Spouse

With the benefit gained from many years of personal experience and contact with dozens of my students, let me offer a series of suggestions which I hope may serve to maximize communication about your Jewish home between you and your Jewish spouse.

1. *As soon as possible after your conversion, begin your discussion of what your common Jewish goals are.* I have found that details flow more easily and logically out of a larger context arrived at jointly.

2. *Articulate to your Jewish spouse as clearly as possible and as gradually as possible your emerging sense of Jewish identity.* Avoid surprises (e.g., "I want us to begin keeping kosher tomorrow morning."). No bombshells, please. It's unfair and counterproductive.

3. *Don't deprecate your spouse or his/her family for lack of Jewish knowledge or a level of Jewish observance that does not meet your ideal standards.* You are asking for trouble if you do, and, frankly, it's arrogant. You are who you are, and you will gradually evolve a personal and family Jewish life style. Others will undoubtedly be influenced by your example. Until then, grant others the respect for their persons that you would wish for yourself.

4. *Avoid nonnegotiable demands.* They hardly ever work, and, even when you think you win, you usually lose. Real change comes not through surrender, but as a result of commitment. And commitment emerges from shared aspirations and shared decisions.

5. *Understand how much your spouse has to teach you about ethnic, if not academic, Judaism.* There is a great deal that one learns,

simply as a result of one's having grown up as a Jew. You will come to value this aspect of Jewish identity as an important part of your personal Jewish past. Also be aware, however, that you have much to give your spouse —a new way of seeing Judaism—through your eyes, unencumbered by excessive cynicism, insecurity, and fear. Such mutual sharing can make for a wonderful partnership.

6. *Don't try to do everything at once.* Set small, attainable objectives together, and build upon your successes.

7. *Don't be impatient with yourself.* You are a Jewish newborn, and you need time to grow.

8. *Never give up.* No one ever promised you that being Jewish would be easy. You and your spouse have a new world which you can create, bonding yourselves together as few couples could ever hope to do. Witness the following story which was shared by a Jewish spouse I know well:

"I grew up in an Orthodox home. When I married Shelley, my parents sat shivah for me, and over the years I fell away from Judaism. But then I watched how Shelley loved Judaism, and how our children came to study Judaism and to love it as a result of her influence. This moved me deeply. And then, at my son's bar mitzvah, watching him up on the bimah, reading from the Torah and loving his Judaism so much, I took a silent vow that I would once again become a Jew. Shelley is a Jew by choice. And she has given my Judaism back to me. From that day forward, I, too, became a Jew by choice."

E D

"You have lovingly given us, O God, festivals of joy, holidays, and times of gladness."

FROM THE FESTIVAL *KIDDUSH*

CHAPTER VI

Holidays— Theirs, Ours . . .
and Mine?

"I'll never forget my first Rosh Hashanah. I asked one of my Jewish friends when the first day of Rosh Hashanah was. He turned to me and said, 'The first day of Rosh Hashanah is Tuesday night! And the last day of Rosh Hashanah,' he added, 'ends Thursday afternoon!' He walked away. I stood there in shock."

HAROLD

SUDDENLY you are facing a new way of looking at time. Days begin the night before. Some holidays last a week. Some come in a bewildering clump and some are just plain bewildering. They have peculiar names. There are many new blessings to learn. And except for Thanksgiving (which is blessedly neutral) all your former holidays can no longer be celebrated.

The High Holy Days

People wish you a happy or a sweet year in the fall because now your year has another beginning—a religious and spiritual one. And while Rosh Hashanah is a joyous time—a time of new beginnings, the birthday of the world—it is also a time of longer, solemn synagogue services, with a special prayer book used only at this season and new customs to be learned. I remember thinking, "I'll never have a sweet year. I'll never even understand it!" I remember my first High Holy Day service. I walked in "cold." The service was a relatively traditional one, almost entirely in Hebrew, and I soon felt lost. I tried to follow as best I could, which was not very well. I felt overwhelmed. I felt I was the only one who couldn't follow and understand. The next year I prepared myself by looking at the High Holy Day prayer book (the machzor) ahead of time and reading the notes I found there. It was fascinating, and each succeeding year I remembered more. Melodies and prayers became familiar and, finally, one year, I could honestly say I felt comfortable with the service. A victory indeed, but one which did not come overnight.

A word about High Holy Day tickets. Unlike most Christian churches, Jewish congregations do not have anything akin to the offering plate. In most synagogues, Jews pay an annual membership fee and are thereby entitled to all membership benefits including tickets for Rosh Hashanah and Yom Kippur services. Since virtually all Jews wish to attend services at this season of the year, congregations issue tickets to assure that their members will have first call on a seat for the synagogue worship. Accordingly, while congregations are open to anyone who wishes to pray at every other time of the year, Rosh Hashanah and Yom Kippur services are often restricted to "ticket holders only."

I remember how put off I was at the thought of tickets for religious services. It was so foreign to my way of thinking. Over the years, however, I have come to realize that, although I may still resist the idea of paying to pray, it is the one time of year when the temple is able to assure its continuity, and thereby its potential for service to its members. I have never seen any individual turned away for lack of funds, and, in fact, the synagogues with which I have had the greatest contact have gone out of their way to embrace and include any Jew who wished to be part of the community.

"I remember my first experience at a High Holy Day service. I had just finished my conversion classes, and about all I really knew was the Shehecheyanu prayer. My wife and I walked into the service and suddenly realized that we had forgotten to bring our prayer books. I was very embarrassed and felt totally out of place. What was I doing here! But suddenly I heard the cantor singing the Shehecheyanu. I knew that! I turned and looked at my wife. She was smiling. I started to smile too, because once I heard the Shehecheyanu I knew everything would be all right. A few minutes later, one of the members of the temple gave me a prayer book. From there it was all smooth sailing. I was officially a Jew."

A L

At first, the holidays which occur in the fall—Rosh Hashanah (the New Year), Yom Kippur (the Day of Atonement), Sukot (the Festival of Booths) and Simchat Torah (the Rejoicing in the Law) seemed a total jumble. I knew that one was the New Year and one was the day you didn't eat, but the rest were a hopeless tangle in my mind. Gradually, however, I came to learn about them. And because I was very interested, I kept learning. The more I learned, understood, and experienced, the more I wanted to do. Now we even build our own sukah, something we started about nine or ten years ago. It is so much fun to build, even though we are the most unhandy people. Putting it up, while it's simple, represents a challenge for us. For a week we eat all our meals in it and invite friends over to share it with us. The children often sleep in it. We love the beautiful fragrance of the etrog. We shake the lulav to remind us that God is everywhere. We even have decorations which have become "heirlooms," and every year we are sorry when we have to take the sukah down. Above all, I like the sense of history and rootedness in a tradition which Sukot and the sukah give to me.

> "If you were born Jewish, there is no way that you can understand what it's like to say the Shema in services for the first time. What an incredible victory! It's the sort of thing that my husband always took for granted. For me it was a triumph!"
>
> MELANIE

Sometimes as I sit in our decorated sukah, or as I march around the synagogue on Simchat Torah carrying a Torah scroll, I think back to the time when I walked into those services "cold." I am so glad I didn't give up. Don't you give up either. Today it is all new to you. For now, just try to participate as much as you can. In time, you will find that it all belongs to you. You won't get there in a year, but twelve months later you'll be further along, and certainly even further with each succeeding year.

Passover/Easter

The major Jewish holiday in the spring is Passover (Pesach). This holiday recalls the Exodus from Egypt, a journey from slavery to freedom. It also celebrates the arrival

66

of spring. There are many beautiful and moving customs and traditions involved with Passover, but the central event of this holiday is the seder, a joyous meal during which the story of the deliverance from Egypt is dramatically recounted. Each one of us, in every generation, is enjoined to feel that we personally came out of Egypt. You might not feel this at your first seder. In fact, the whole event may be very confusing: the large group of people, symbolic foods on the table, a staggering amount to eat and drink, and many unfamiliar songs.

"My first seder was a real disaster. I invited my parents and my husband's parents. I told my parents several times that Passover was a time when Jews didn't eat bread and I asked them not to bring any, since my mother loves to bake bread. My parents arrived, and, though my mother didn't bring any bread, she did hand me something that she had baked that morning—a cake!"

KAREN

"I really liked my first seder, though I wanted it to be more formal. I can remember the taste of the wine, and everything being new. I was bothered, however, by how fast everyone was speaking Hebrew. I knew how to follow the Latin in the church service. But the Hebrew intimidated me. They read it so fast, it was hard to understand. How could it possibly have any meaning? Now I know better."

RICHARD

One way to survive a seder is to arrive hungry. (My first seder came right on the heels of Easter dinner at my parents, and I thought I'd never make it!) Another is to read through a haggadah (the book which contains the seder service) beforehand. If you can, find out which haggadah will be used at your seder. Then go to a Jewish bookstore a few weeks before Passover. You will see several kinds of haggadahs. They might be very different from one another. Look through a number of them, then buy a copy of "your" haggadah. Take it home and become familiar with it. If you can find them, get records or tapes of the principal songs and prayers of the seder and listen to them as well. You don't have to make your own seder at the beginning. Instead, get yourself invited to one where you can watch and participate. Eventually, you'll be ready to lead your own.

What about your family and Easter? As we have already discussed, it is perfectly acceptable to visit them and wish them a happy Easter. It is fine to join them for Easter dinner. Families should be together for holidays. However, it is important to make the distinction in your own mind that *you are with them as they celebrate.* It is not your holiday to celebrate in your home. Although I had happy memories of Easter, they were centered principally around the family gathering at dinner. Since I could still do that comfortably, I didn't feel a great sense of loss. The most difficult time for me, as it is for most of those who convert, came not in the spring but in the winter.

Chanukah/Christmas

"I remember my first Chanukah after my conversion. Sure I lit the candles, but I really didn't feel I knew enough about Chanukah to make it meaningful. I didn't know the context. My husband didn't get too excited about Chanukah either, and that didn't help. It was a big disappointment. Then came Christmas. On Christmas eve, I turned on the radio and there were Christmas carols playing. I just dissolved in tears. It was only then that I realized what I was missing. It wasn't the gifts and it wasn't the tree. I was missing the sense of family. I was missing my mother, and the smells in the house, and the music. The problem was that my husband didn't think of Chanukah in those terms at all. He bought me a Christmas tree! I was furious. Now I know better. Chanukah can be just as much a family holiday as Christmas used to be in my life. And the meaning of Chanukah is so much a part of me now that it's hard to believe that my first Chanukah and my first Christmas after my conversion were so painful."

PRISCILLA

Christmas! How could I not have Christmas? The happiest memories of my life were bound up with it. Smells, colors, sounds—it was so much a part of my consciousness. I was resentful at the thought of having to give it up. But I did come to the realization that a Christmas tree would have no place in my Jewish home. At first I felt a void and a sense of sadness, which intensified when the annual Christmas advertising and selling blitz began. As December 25th drew nearer, I felt deprived. I was a sudden outsider in my own culture. Suddenly, I understood what it meant to be a minority. Where was "my" holiday? Where were the blazing signs that said "Happy Chanukah"? Every once in a while I would see a little one somewhere and I would silently rejoice. I became angry at this majority culture which pushed Christmas so relentlessly and profitably. I wanted equal time, space, and recognition for "my" holiday, Chanukah. But Chanukah didn't yet feel like my holiday. I felt in limbo between the two, not belonging anywhere and feeling guilty about feeling like that.

It is important for you to realize that Chanukah is not a Jewish Christmas. It should not become a compensation for the loss of Christmas in your own life. It is not about

69

buying silver and blue wrapping paper instead of red and green, or Chanukah decorations instead of Christmas wreaths. It is a completely different holiday, and you must learn about it so that you can celebrate it on its own terms. Chanukah has important values to teach—dedication, religious freedom, the triumph of the few over the many, crucial values for any society, values embodied in your Judaism.

As I *felt* more Jewish, my feelings of loss diminished. Although I still had my happy childhood Christmas memories, I didn't have room for Christmas in my Jewish present. I could appreciate it, and be with my family, and even open the Christmas presents they gave me, but it was no longer mine. Christmas presents? Yes. Every year my family gives Christmas presents to my husband, my children, and me. It makes them feel good. It is their expression of love and sharing. I could ask them to call them "Chanukah presents" and wrap them in Chanukah paper, but I don't feel I have to make my statement that way. Although we often go to my family for Christmas dinner, they know that in our home we celebrate Chanukah. This has been established over the years. In fact, they come to our house to see the menorah lit and to eat latkes with us. In this way, we all get pleasure while respecting each other's ways and choices. The distinction is maintained. My children know they are Jews because their parents are Jews, they live in a Jewish home, they receive a Jewish education, and with us they go to the synagogue. But they also realize that half of their family (whom they also love very much) is Christian. There is no feeling of division and competition. My children know they are Jews. They are not unhappy because they don't celebrate Christmas and Easter. Neither are they confused. As a matter of fact, almost exactly the opposite is true. My daughter Naomi goes to a Jewish day school, and there-fore is used to the rhythms of the Jewish calendar. Juda-ism is so much a part of her life that after a recent Thanks-giving she asked me "What date is Christmas this year?" Since the Jewish calendar is a lunar calendar, Jewish holi-days fall at a different time every year on the Gregorian calendar. Because my teenage daughter is so used to the rhythms of the Jewish calendar, she assumed that all holi-days were that way. I don't worry any more about Naomi confusing Christmas and Chanukah.

All these clarifications are easy to write about, but they are sometimes difficult to achieve, especially at the begin-ning. Your family might feel in some way that they have lost you. In order to minimize those fears it is important for you to spend their holidays with them. It might be easy for you to do this, for it might diminish your own feelings of loss as well. But it also may be difficult to establish and maintain your new identity under those circumstances. It will take time, but it will come. In the beginning, you may feel trapped between two worlds and at home in neither. And it is never easy to present yourself as different to your parents, who see you the way they have always seen you, although you may no longer be that way. It took me a long time to be comfortable with my difference from my family, and it took them an equally long time to make their adjustment. It is impor-tant to keep reestablishing your identity once you've dealt with your own ambivalence. You can then present yourself unambivalently to them. In time, I hope that your family, like mine, will come to respect your decisions and your choice.

In the meantime, immerse yourself in Chanukah. Buy a chanukiah (menorah) and invite friends over for candle-lighting. Make latkes. Learn to spin a dreidel. Sing! And

71

especially, come to appreciate this holiday of dedication and freedom which embodies an important lesson for our society—the possibility that the few *can* make a difference in the face of overwhelming odds.

Shabbat—An Island in Time

You will discover the joy of celebrating many other Jewish holidays during the course of the year. You will come to know the customs, foods, and ceremonies associated with each. But there is a holiday which comes every week and is, perhaps, the most special of all—Shabbat, the Sabbath. Shabbat reminds us weekly of two things: the wonder of the world's creation and the fact that God brought the Jewish people out of Egypt, from slavery to freedom. Shabbat also provides us with a weekly opportunity for personal re-creation. On this one day, we can stop, be free from our weekly cares and concerns, and create a special place for us and our families to *be*. Indeed, Jewish tradition teaches that each of us is given an extra soul on every Shabbat so that we might savor the uniqueness of Shabbat.

How do we do this? Is it possible? Yes, it is possible. But Shabbat observance does not happen all at once, automatically. Like anything else worthwhile, it takes time and practice.

First, you must make the commitment to "doing Shabbat." Then decide how to begin. You may want to start by memorizing the candle blessing. Once you've accomplished that, you can move on to the Friday night Kiddush or the blessing over the chalah. If you can read the Hebrew, fine. If not, work from a transliteration. Learn it a sentence at a time. Don't expect to feel comfortable reciting the blessing the first time you do it. As you recite the blessing week after week, it will become part of you. It will become yours.

Develop a weekly routine of cleaning and straightening up the house so that it is neat and special for Shabbat. While cleaning, cooking, or doing chores, play a tape or record of Shabbat blessings and songs. You will learn them very quickly and will enjoy your work a little more as a bonus.

Buy some flowers. Try making a kugel or some favorite or special food. The important thing to remember is that it is best to begin with one small skill. Master that, then add another.

Because Shabbat comes every week, you will get a great deal of practice. The blessings are not very difficult, and they contain most of the words of blessings which are said on other holidays and other Jewish occasions. In addition, there are resources which are readily available and which will be especially helpful to you in mastering Shabbat. Consult the bibliography at the end of this book for a few of the most accessible books and records.

Above all, as your Shabbat "repertoire" grows, use it every week. Then your preparation will truly become part of your life, and you will have begun to establish Shabbat as a regular part of your week. I have found that it is the most indispensable and valuable part of every seven days of my life. My children know that Friday night is a time when we will all be together, a family time which is different from the rush and sometime hysteria of the week. We often like to invite friends for Shabbat dinner, but it is just as lovely for the four of us to be by ourselves and have the luxury of time away from everyone else.

Although I am tired by the time Friday night arrives, when I sit in the light of my Shabbat candles, I experience a feeling of happiness which I hope you will know as well. I love the warm family feeling, the sense of continuing a tradition, and the personal sense of fulfillment which I feel in creating beautiful memories for myself and for my children.

One final suggestion. Judaism has a special way of marking those moments in our lives when we accomplish something new. It is the Shehecheyanu prayer. If you don't know it, learn it. It's simple and easy to memorize. It is a prayer which expresses thanks to God for our having lived long enough to experience something special. Indeed, if your experience is like mine, every new accomplishment, Jewishly speaking, will be extra special. And you, like me, may wish to mark that time by reciting the Shehecheyanu. I urge you to try it. Perhaps the Shehecheyanu can be your very first Jewish skill.

Shehecheyanu

בָּרוּךְ אַתָּה יְיָ אֱלֹהֵינוּ מֶלֶךְ הָעוֹלָם שֶׁהֶחֱיָנוּ וְקִיְּמָנוּ וְהִגִּיעָנוּ לַזְּמַן הַזֶּה.

Baruch Atah Adonai Elohenu, Melech haolam, shehecheyanu, vekiyemanu, vehigianu lazman hazeh.

74

Blessed is the Lord our God, Ruler of the universe, for giving us life, for sustaining us, and for enabling us to reach for this season.

Ritual Objects You Might Wish to Begin Collecting

Shabbat

— To welcome Shabbat:
- Candlesticks
- Shabbat candles
- Kiddush cup
- Chalah cover
- Chalah board or tray

You may also wish to find an especially pretty tablecloth. Although white is traditional, you may use any color.

— For Havdalah:
- A spice box or a glass or pottery dish to hold Havdalah spices. Cloves are often used, though any sweet smelling spice is appropriate. You may eventually want to buy an entire Havdalah set. To begin with, you can use a dish for spices and your Kiddush cup for the wine.
- A braided Havdalah candle

Chanukah

- A Chanukah menorah
- Chanukah candles
- Dreidel

Passover

- A Passover seder plate, with special places on it for all the symbols of the holiday
- A matzah cover

A mezuzah to put on your front door

Most of these items are available in temple gift shops. You will also find them in stores which specialize in Judaica.

"For every thing there is a season . . . a time to be born and a time to die."

ECCLESIASTES

CHAPTER VII

The Jewish Life Cycle

BIRTH, reaching adulthood, marriage, death—the life cycle—are all peak moments which mark a transition from one stage of life to another. With the exception of death, these peak moments are occasions for joy and celebration in every major religious tradition, and are accompanied by distinctive customs and ceremonies. Judaism has evolved unique rituals to commemorate these key moments. For you, the ways of the Jewish life cycle present enormous potential for both fulfillment and frustration.

Sometimes, in a family in which there is another religion represented, life-cycle events can be a painful reminder of differences and division. But they can also provide opportunities for you to make connections and to embrace those who are near and dear to you.

Whether we are discussing birth, bar/bat mitzvah, or marriage (we will deal with death separately), there are three principles which apply to all Jewish life-cycle events in relation to your non-Jewish family:

1. *Include* your non-Jewish family in all Jewish life-cycle celebrations.

2. *Explain* as much as possible about the life-cycle event to your non-Jewish family—in advance.

3. *Involve* your non-Jewish family in every Jewish life-cycle celebration in some appropriate way.

The first two principles are relatively straightforward. First, make sure that your family is included in any special life-cycle event. Invite them well ahead of time. If they are coming in from out of town, see that they are comfortably situated.

Next, explain to them what will be happening—in advance! Don't surprise them. It would be very helpful to give them some reading material a month or two before the actual celebration and answer questions they might have. Any number of books listed in the bibliography at the back of this book will be fine, but I particularly recommend the *Jewish Home* series (UAHC). There are close to a dozen *Jewish Home* booklets currently in print, and a complete set makes a lovely and practical gift for any non-Jewish or Jewish family. They are clear, succinct, and to the point.

Now we come to the third—*and most important*—element in approaching life-cycle events—involvement of the non-Jewish family. The challenge is to find appropriate participatory roles for family members which neither embarrass nor patronize them. Here are just a few ideas.

Marriage

The family can and should be involved in every phase of your wedding preparations, from the planning to the actual ceremony itself. During the wedding, your non-Jewish family can walk down the aisle with you. They can stand under the chupah. They can be "ring bearers" or wedding attendants. One rabbi I know asks both the Jewish and non-Jewish parents to bless the bride and groom quietly just prior to concluding the ceremony. Another rabbi makes a point of designating members of both the Jewish and non-Jewish families to hold the supports for each of the four corners of the chupah.

Birth

"Each child brings its own blessing into the world."
Talmud

The birth of a child is indeed a blessing and a joy to share with your families. If physically possible, both sets of grandparents should be present at the temple naming ceremony, and should jointly host an Oneg Shabbat in honor of their grandchild. At the ceremony of berit milah (circumcision), your parents can hold the baby prior to the ritual. They can join in reciting the Shehecheyanu, in Hebrew with some preparation, or in English. At the celebration following the ritual, they can propose a toast or offer a prayer for their new-born grandchild. Exactly the same options exist in the case of the naming of a daughter, especially if you choose to have the ceremony of berit hachayim which is now part of the Reform movement's normative ritual.

Bar/Bat Mitzvah

My family enjoyed "our" bar mitzvah, and they enjoyed their participation in it. Eight months prior to the bar mitzvah, they made their airline reservations. They were taking no chances! Once safely in Los Angeles, they pitched in, helping to cook and keep everything under control. They loved the service. Proudly, they came up to open the ark. They wept with pride as I was called to the Torah for an aliyah. They beamed as David chanted his blessings. During the service, my husband Ben and I spoke to David, reflecting not only on his beginnings but on our own as well. We, along with our families, cried and laughed and were filled to overflowing with the complex mixture of feelings that come at special times marking passages from one stage of life to another.

A bar/bat mitzvah service presents many opportunities for your family's participation, depending on the custom of your synagogue. Your family might read certain English sections of the service, join in reciting the Shehecheyanu, or offer a special prayer for their grandchild. In the course of your planning the service with the rabbi, you should be sure to discuss your desire to have maximum involvement on the part of your family.

There were extra touches which enriched David's bar mitzvah immeasurably. My family is Italian. For the invitation, therefore, I found a picture of the young King David holding his harp, from an eighteenth-century Italian folk art haggadah and duly noted the provenance on the back of the invitation. We made certain, long before the party, that our band could play tarantellas and a couple of other Italian songs as well as the predominantly Jewish/Israeli music in which they specialized. When, during the party, the band struck up a tarantella, my family was surprised, then delighted. In an instant they were up and leading everyone in a dance which went on and on and on. My very Italian family was totally at home at "our" bar mitzvah. And so was I!

All of the suggestions I have set forth in this chapter thus far are offered to you from the perspective of many years, and with the benefit of hindsight. I must confess that at my wedding, and at my son's berit milah, I did not feel secure enough, either in experience or in knowledge, to do any of the things that I now propose to you. That did not happen until "our" bar mitzvah. I often regret the missed opportunities for family togetherness which I might have engendered with a little planning. I hope that these suggestions will provide a "shortcut" for you, a shortcut which I could not see when I began my life as a Jew.

When a Parent Dies

Perhaps the single most difficult moment of my Jewish life occurred when my father died. The death of a parent is always painful, and serves as a catalyst for the release of deep and powerful emotions. This I knew. But I was totally unprepared for the range of feelings I experienced, and the confusion that suddenly engulfed me eight years after my conversion, long after I thought I had become quite comfortable with my Jewish identity.

My father died on the second day of Passover. My brother and I flew to Philadelphia for the funeral service, and I suddenly felt totally disoriented and alone. I had come cross country from my Passover seder to my Christian father's funeral. Surroundings once so familiar seemed somehow strange. I helped arrange a funeral service whose ritual was completely at variance with my own Jewish beliefs. I reentered the church in which I was raised, so well known to me, yet so removed from me. During this pre-Easter week, I listened to my family's minister speak of my father and of the resurrection, and the better place to which he had gone. These were comforting words to many, but not to me. And even as the service ended, with the choir singing his favorite hymn which I had always sung to him as a little girl, I realized that I could find no comfortable way in which to mourn my own father.

In the home of my childhood, alone, with none of my Jewish friends and community around me, I could not sit shivah or recite Kaddish. I felt that I had gone back in time and space. Indeed, to this very day, I still have not resolved the situation to my own satisfaction.

How does one mourn a non-Jewish parent, respecting a mother's or father's religious beliefs while still easing one's personal grief? I have no easy answers. I can only tell you what I have done. I say the Yizkor prayer for my father but do not light a yahrzeit candle. On the anniversary of his death, I make a contribution to his church in his name and I recite a psalm in his memory. Other Jews by choice I know have handled their need to mourn in similar ways. One especially dear friend who lost her mother was fortunate in having a deeply sensitive cantor. Knowing that the funeral service was to be held in a

Protestant church, the cantor called ahead of time and arranged to participate in the service by singing the 23rd Psalm. This was an act of great sensitivity, which reassured my friend and her children. They saw that even in this unusually difficult moment they were not alone. Their Jewish "community" was there for them and with them as they mourned their beloved grandmother. After the service, my friend sat shivah and said Kaddish for a year for her mother. This was her way.

Almost invariably, students in classes that I teach raise the question of that ultimate need to mourn a parent authentically and sensitively. They raise the issue with great anxiety, and I answer them with the same thought that I now share with you. God willing, our parents will enjoy long, happy, and productive lives. But when the end comes, as it must for all of us, all that anyone can ask or expect is that we will do our best. In the midst of our own grief, we will try to be true to them and to do what they believed. Beyond that, nothing can be asked. Beyond that, nothing can be promised.

"One who is descended from you often teaches you."

FROM THE *TALMUD*

CHAPTER VIII

Children

"I remember the day my daughter came home from school, beaming. A classmate of hers had told another student that that student's mother was not really Jewish because she was a convert. My daughter, who at the time was all of nine years old, stood up and reprimanded the other student. 'You don't know what you're talking about,' she said. 'Her mother is Jewish. And she's *really* Jewish because she *chose* to be Jewish! And my mom is Jewish too. She chose to be Jewish, and she knows more than almost any Jewish person I know—including rabbis!' For my daughter, that moment was one of the proudest of her life. I think it was also one of the proudest of mine."

RACHEL

YOUR CHILDREN will be your teachers. There is nothing that can help you understand and clarify your beliefs more than trying to explain them to your children.

Your decision to be a Jew will affect no one's life more profoundly than that of your child. And therein lies the single greatest challenge to one who has chosen Judaism, for in embracing Judaism you have destroyed a part of your parents' expectations for your future as well as their vision of the continuity of the entire family.

I have posed the problem in such a candid fashion

because it is real. It must be addressed, in spite of the anxiety, pain, and hurt that may occur at the very beginning of that process.

> "I was surprised, in looking over my monthly phone bill, to find what appeared to be an excessive number of long distance calls to my parents' home. That night at dinner, I learned a lesson. My son shamefacedly admitted that he had made the calls, and said to me, 'Daddy, I love grandma and grandpa. Just because you're mad at them, it isn't fair that I shouldn't have a grandma and grandpa.' It started a process that eventually led to a family reconciliation."
>
> M A U R Y

The first thing to attend to is *your* relationship with your parents. If that relationship is marked by tension and bitterness, *make no mistake;* your children will be aware of it. In presenting this discussion, then, I must assume that you have set into motion a mechanism for dealing with the concerns which we treated more fully in Chapter III. You do not need to have all the problems resolved. That will require a period of months, perhaps years. But you do need to have begun the process.

Next, and *crucial!* Always remember that your children will come into the world knowing nothing of the background of your conversion. Like all children, their primary concern will be a need for security and love, derived first from parents, and secondly from grandparents. It can be terribly confusing and hurtful to children when they must choose between those whom they love, when they sense distance or receive conflicting signals as to who they are, or when they feel that life is a contest with them as the prize.

"My parents never approved of my conversion. In fact, we have not spoken since the day I became a Jew. My son has enjoyed a beautiful relationship with my in-laws, but at the age of six, sensing that something was wrong, he approached me one day and asked, 'Mommy, don't you have parents too?' It was a very difficult day in my life. I tried to explain the situation as best I could given his age and level of understanding. It still hurt, though. And there has been no happy ending."

SOPHIA

So much for philosophy. Having accepted the premises I have outlined, how do you go about creating a home environment in which it is possible to have two religious traditions represented and respected, and at the same time make it absolutely clear that Judaism is "yours"? I suggest the following six-step plan:

1. *Clarify your own Jewish identity.*

As we have already discussed, this is a gradual process. The more you do, the more authentic you will feel. And it is only when you have made a personal commitment to a Jewish "self" that you can credibly convey that sense of self to others, particularly to your children.

2. *Create a Jewish home.*

Your personal choice affirmed, make your house a Jewish home. Observe holidays. Light Shabbat candles. Chant the Kiddush. Recite Hamotsi. Make Havdalah. Have Jewish books and ritual objects on your shelves. Affix a mezuzah to your door. In short, allow the outward man-

88

ifestations of Judaism to reflect what is already an inner reality.

3. Help your non-Jewish family understand clearly what it means to have a Jewish home, what goes on there, and the limits that they must respect and observe.

Your family, for example, should know that you will be observing only Jewish holidays in your home from this point on. If you have decided to have a kosher kitchen, your family should know what that means so that they don't come to visit you bringing food that will not be permissible, and thereby embarrassing both you and them.

I remember that after we decided to change our kitchen to a kosher kitchen, my mother, who loves to cook, was afraid to touch anything! She felt uncomfortable, and angry, too, because she considered this to be "extreme" Jewish behavior. I explained to her how to cook in a kosher kitchen. And now? Now the highlight of her every visit is a pasta cooking and eating "workshop" for my daughter and her classmates from the Hebrew day school—in *her* daughter's kosher kitchen! She still balks at not putting cheese in the meatballs, but she beams at the kids and their terrific appetites and how sweet they are. Furthermore, in the day school itself, "Naomi's Grandma" has become a legend—the only grandma in the world who can make spaghetti from eggs, water, and flour!

*4.   Find ways to be with your family in their home for holidays
—but not as a celebrant of those holidays.*

Be prepared, however, for tricky moments. When my
son David was five years old, we made a special trip
East to be with my parents in Philadelphia. We prepared David very carefully for the trip, explaining to
him that we were going to "be with" grandma and
grandpa on "their holiday," that we were Jewish and
observed Chanukah, but that this was still a family
occasion in which all of us could participate. One of
the special treats that my mother had planned for me
—and for herself—was a luncheon with her fellow
workers at a Philadelphia office. She walked in with
David, the proud grandma. She introduced him to her
friends, who were, of course, all dressed up for this
special Christmas event. One of her friends leaned
down to David and said to him, "Hello, David. Merry
Christmas!" My son merely stared at her and replied:
"We don't observe Christmas." The woman was mor-
tified. My mother was embarrassed. But it all worked
out fine in the end. With the passing of the years, this
incident has become one of those precious family stories that is retold time and time again on an annual
basis.

5.   Be together as much a possible at other, non-holiday times.

This strengthens the family relationship and reassures
everyone. Do your best to be together on birthdays, anni-
versaries, other non-religious celebrations, or just for a
day or a weekend. At times like these, everyone comes to

realize that there is much more that unites than divides. Though thousands of miles may separate you from your family, a fact of life for many of us today, I urge you to keep this goal of "nonthreatening togetherness" as a priority. It pays handsome dividends.

6. Finally, all the principles embodied in these steps must be conveyed to your children.

But—children are quick to understand. They have extremely sensitive antennae, so don't be surprised if they understand your unspoken actions long before you articulate anything to them. If you begin the process I have just outlined, they will receive very clear messages from you. If you know who *you* are, you will transmit that to your children as a function of your very being. Therefore, any discussions you have with your children will take place in a context of prior understanding.

That is the process. We can reduce it to several steps on paper, but obviously it is hardly as simple or as self-contained as that. Clearly there will be variables and variations in the process from family to family. Sometimes parents will be understanding, perhaps even very receptive from the very beginning. In a very few instances, parents may try to compete religiously for the children. Those cases are most difficult, and when they occur you will have to assess your personal situation and act accordingly.

"When my husband and I went away, we left the children with my parents. On Sunday morning, they took my son to church with them, and, almost in passing, asked him if he would like

91

to become a member of their church. Adam, who was six years old, didn't want to disappoint his grandma and grandpa and said yes. When we returned home, he told us the entire story. I was furious! More than that, I was hurt. I think it was the first time in my life that I ever confronted my parents. They finally understood that I was serious about my Judaism, but to this day my son is listed as a member of the First Presbyterian Church."

MARGARET

You must be sensitive to everyone's feelings and not convey the implicit message that one side is winning and one side is losing. Your conversion should never be seen in those terms. Yet, you *have* made a choice, and that very fact implies that there will be a difference in your life. Yours will be a Jewish home, because that's what *you* are. That's the kind of life *you* will lead. Accordingly, you will have to make an extra effort to include, rather than exclude, your family in your Judaism. It may be difficult to do, especially at first, since you will be struggling to include them while you are still defining who you are. But it's worth the effort. Family is central to all our lives.

What is the ultimate goal? I think I can illustrate it through a personal family experience that occurred recently. My fourteen-year-old son David, having come to know his non-Jewish family as a result of a beautiful bar mitzvah experience, decided to spend an entire month with them, working and sharing that time with his non-Jewish aunts and uncles and of course with his grandmother. Naturally, I had great reservations about sending him off all alone, but I needn't have been anxious at all. Not only was it a productive experience in terms of work, but he established strong personal relationships with my mother and my sister. Religious differences were not even a factor in that growing relationship. They related as one person to another, one loving relative to another, happy to be together, and happy to share in a common summer experience. David returned after his trip truly knowing my family for the first time. He has his own identity as a member of my family. Knowing exactly who he is as a Jew, he is able to love and embrace his non-Jewish family as his own.

"A community is too heavy for any one person to carry alone."

FROM THE *MIDRASH*

"Do not separate yourself from the community."

FROM THE *MISHNAH*

CHAPTER IX

Your Jewish Community

JUDAISM is more than holidays, more than rabbis, more than new family and friends. Judaism also includes a whole new community, places you'll want to go, and people you'll want to meet.

While the size of your city will often determine how rich the local resources available to you will be, here are some you'll want to look for:

1. Reform synagogue
2. Conservative synagogue
3. Orthodox synagogue
4. Reconstructionist synagogue

In addition to providing worship services, synagogues can be a valuable resource for education, both formal and informal. Lecture series, Hebrew classes, dance, cooking, Bible, Jewish history and observance are often offered as part of a congregation's adult education program. Temples frequently sponsor adult or family weekends and many other Jewish experiential events. Visit your local congregation. Decide which one you'd like to join, and become a member.

5. Jewish bakery
6. Jewish butcher shop

7. Jewish bookstores—They also stock religious articles such as mezuzahs, Shabbat candles, candlesticks, and menorahs as well as records and tapes. In the bookstore, as we have already noted, you will be able to browse through different prayer books, Bibles, and haggadahs. You can also find a variety of books on all aspects of Judaism.

8. Jewish gift shop (sometimes located in synagogues)

9. Jewish museum—If you have a Jewish museum in your community, it can be an extremely valuable educational resource for you. In addition to the permanent and temporary exhibitions, museums also frequently have lovely gift shops. They generally have one or more lecture series and a wide range of educational opportunities for both adults and children. Los Angeles, New York, Washington, D.C., Chicago, Philadelphia, and Berkeley, California, all have major Jewish museums. In addition, many congregations throughout the United States have fine collections of Judaic items.

10. Jewish delicatessen—For all those foods you've heard about but not yet sampled yourself.

11. Any synagogue library—Good for browsing. You can often check books out of the library, whether or not you are a member of that particular synagogue.

12. Jewish community center—Often a cultural center for the Jewish community. The center frequently offers programs of Jewish education, camping, contemporary issues, child care, and recreation.

13. Jewish day school

14. Federation of Jewish Philanthropies/United Jewish Appeal—Central fund-raising agency of the Jewish community, a single address like Community Chest. Most

members of the Jewish community make a gift to Federation/UJA, which in turn appropriates funds to local, national, and international Jewish causes. In many cities, especially large ones, Federation also works in tandem with other local congregations and Jewish agencies in providing programs and services for all segments of the community.

15. Bureau of Jewish Education
16. Anti-Defamation League of B'nai B'rith
17. American Jewish Committee
18. American Jewish Congress

The last three listings are Jewish "defense" organizations which were organized primarily to monitor American governmental policy as it relates to the Jewish community, to pursue legal battles where necessary to establish Jewish rights, to alert the Jewish community to possible sources of anti-Semitism domestically, and to mobilize the American Jewish community to resist such prejudice. You will also often read of ADL, the American Jewish Committee, and the American Jewish Congress joining with other, non-Jewish agencies in Supreme Court cases which touch on universal human rights as well as particular Jewish issues.

19. Jewish National Fund—Undertakes the forestation and development of land in the State of Israel. Jews in every country of the world plant tens of thousands of trees annually through gifts to the JNF. You can obtain the historic JNF "blue box" (tsedakah box) for your home at no charge from the local or the national office of the Jewish National Fund.

20. Local branches of Jewish organizations such as the National Federation of Temple Brotherhoods, National Federation of Temple Sisterhoods, Hadassah,

ORT, B'nai B'rith, and the National Council of Jewish Women—Contact the local representative for further information.

21. Jewish home for the aged
22. Local university Jewish studies department
23. Local college B'nai B'rith Hillel Foundation—The "Hillel House" on any college campus serves as a gathering place for Jewish students as well as one of the only places on campus where students can obtain kosher meals. In addition, Hillel sponsors Shabbat services and many educational programs throughout the year.
24. Rabbis
25. Cantors
26. Jewish educators
27. Local library
28. Jewish antiquities store

You will also want to write to the national offices of the Union of American Hebrew Congregations (Reform) and the United Synagogue of America (Conservative) for details regarding their national and regional programs in the areas of social action; college and high school youth; summer camps; Israel study programs; adult education; parent and family education; nursery, religious school, and day school education; publications; audio-visual materials; and other services. The addresses are:

Union of American Hebrew Congregations
838 Fifth Avenue
New York, New York 10021
United Synagogues of America
155 Fifth Avenue
New York, New York 10010

Welcome to your new community. There are lots of new people out there who can make a difference in your life. Many of the organizations I have described need, want, and indeed survive with the assistance of concerned individuals who volunteer their time. Try it! Donating your time and energy to a Jewish organization is a very special kind of tsedakah. In the process, you will meet new people, feel your contribution firsthand, and truly become a part of your new community. All that's required is for you to take the first step. Good luck!

From Others Who Have Been There

"Before I was a Jew, I didn't realize that there was a Jewish community. Now I know it's there. Somewhere, some part of me wants to be in the Jewish community. I just don't know where yet. I realize that there are lots of parts to a Jewish community, and some places where I would feel very comfortable. I just haven't found it yet. But I will."

GEORGE

"I'm going to look around my community for a place where I can study a little bit more. I'm still insecure. I feel I do not know enough yet. When do you really know enough to be a full-fledged Jew?"

WALTER

"One thing that I am doing is to belong to a Jewish federation that's developing leaders to move into Jewish organizations. They are afraid that young people are not coming in, so they are training us. That will be my way of becoming involved in the Jewish community. I like that. It's not just giving money, but also giving time. I like to learn by giving the time and by seeing where the money goes."

ANITA

99

"I would really like to become involved in what I do. I really want to be doing things. I don't just want to be a bystander. So when I join a temple, I hope that I won't feel too strange. Because I really want to fit in."

PATRICE

"Those who bring others near to Judaism are accorded the same merit as though they had given birth to them."

BERESHIT RABBAH

CHAPTER X

Let's Look to the Future—Together

"Judaism offers life, not death. It teaches free will, not surrender of body and soul to another human being. The Jew prays directly to God, not through an intermediary who stands between him and his God. Judaism is a religion of hope and not despair; it insists that man and society are perfectible. Judaism has an enormous amount of wisdom and experience to offer this troubled world, and we Jews ought to be proud to speak about it, frankly, freely, and with dignity."

Rabbi Alexander M. Schindler
Presidential address to the UAHC
Board of Trustees
December 2, 1978 (Houston, Texas)

THE FOLLOWING chapter is written both for Jews by choice and for congregational leaders. All of us who have worked with rabbis and members of the temple staff and Board of Trustees recognize that we, Jews by choice, can be of immeasurable help in creating a congregational program that will ensure a warm welcome to those who have chosen Judaism.

Through this chapter, then, we hope to create a team— a team of people sharing common goals and beliefs—who can work together to attain goals and realize cherished dreams.

Rabbi Schindler's stirring words called into being a comprehensive program of Outreach to Jews by choice, the intermarried, and those who are in search of a meaningful faith. Rabbi Schindler's address was greeted with banner headlines, newspaper editorials, and magazine articles, overwhelmingly positive in tone. It was clear that the Outreach vision touched and moved great numbers of Jews on the deepest emotional level.

But if Outreach is to be real, if the dream is to be fulfilled, the sentiments expressed so powerfully in Rabbi Schindler's Houston address must find expression in concrete programatic efforts. Therefore, in this concluding chapter I address myself to the entire Jewish community of North America, whether Jews by birth or Jews by choice, in the hope that you will carefully examine the programatic possibilities that follow and implement them in your community. The suggestions that follow constitute an overall blueprint of congregational projects and programs which I believe can be implemented at once, which are fully integrated, and which embody an overall vision rather than a piecemeal approach. They represent a first step on the road to a sensitive and caring response to the newest members of our ancient faith.

Eight Programs for Jews by Choice

1. Sensitizing the temple staff.

The conversion process begins the moment a person picks up a telephone or walks into the temple office and inquires about the process of conversion. Therefore, a first step in our efforts must be to sensitize our congregational staff members, to help them understand how difficult it often is to make that first phone call, and to guide them in responding warmly and supportively. Though it is a warm and wonderful place to us, a temple can seem strange and eerie to one who is entering it for the first time. By being aware of those natural and normal human emotions, and discussing how best to alleviate anxiety and fear, we can be a source of support.

2. Consciousness-raising programs for the rabbi.

Rabbis, too, must remember that many of those who come to them to inquire about conversion feel nervous, inadequate, and somehow on trial. Those who have never met a rabbi have no idea how to approach him or her. Is the rabbi like a priest? Is the rabbi supposedly infallible? Is the rabbi going to be a harsh judge? These and other questions run through the mind of any person who sits in the alcove of a rabbi's office waiting for that initial meeting. The sense of anxiety is only heightened as one enters a rabbi's office for the first time, confronting bookcases from floor to ceiling and an environment which can be formidable at best. Even before coming to know the rabbi as a person, therefore, the potential new Jew may be afraid and ill at ease.

It would be helpful to bring together those who have chosen Judaism in your congregation so that they can discuss their candid reactions to the rabbi's approach, their feelings about their relationship with the rabbi or rabbis with whom they worked during their conversion, as well as what they perceived as the most helpful things the rabbi did and the most disturbing as well. This frank sharing could then be used as a basis of discussion with the rabbi, both as means of indicating support for the rabbi's efforts and as a way of helping the rabbi make his or her work with Jews by choice even more effective.

3.   Rename your "conversion" classes.

Stop referring to courses of study leading to conversion as "conversion" classes. Instead, they should be called "introduction to Judaism" classes and should be opened to the entire congregation. Redefined in this manner, they can serve as a point of entry into Judaism for those who are in the process of becoming Jews, as well as a point of re-entry for born-Jews whose Jewish education was inadequate. There are many born-Jews who need such a course, and who would welcome it as a valuable part of their self-education as Jews.

4.   Evaluate your introduction to Judaism curriculum carefully.

Most introduction to Judaism classes, whether on a congregational or community level, tend to be heavily

105

weighted in the direction of cognitive material. This leads to an academic, but passive, knowledge of Judaism.

Where this is the case, we often see the phenomenon of "post-pedagogic paralysis." Those who have come to Judaism know facts, figures, and dates but have no idea how to function as Jews, or that there are resources available to them in their new Jewish setting. Consequently, they "do" little or nothing! I urge a more active, experiential approach to Judaism through our introductory courses. Have students visit a Jewish bookstore, bakery, butcher shop, other synagogues in the community, and places of Jewish interests in general. Conduct a Passover seder. Arrange for all class members to go to Shabbat services together, preceded by a group Shabbat dinner at the temple. Teach Jewish songs as part of each class. In short, *celebrate* Judaism! This is not *instead* of a cognitive approach, but *together with it.* While introductory classes in Judaism, as in any subject, can only do so much, they should prepare those in them to *live* and *do* Jewishly.

I hope that in time every introduction to Judaism course will last at least eighteen weeks. I hope that each will deal with the facts *and* feelings of Judaism, and also with the very real problems which Jews by choice face in relating to two sets of families, two sets of holidays, and the feelings of loss so often associated with conversion. A facility in Hebrew reading is essential. At least one camp weekend would be ideal. But, above all, I urge you always to emphasize the fact that choosing Judaism is a beginning. An introduction to Judaism course is just that. Becoming Jewish is a *process* that will extend over the course of a lifetime.

5.   Consider the possibility of public conversion ceremonies.

I have already described my own conversion ceremony, a small and quiet ritual in the rabbi's study. I believe, however, that we must begin to encourage the option of public conversion ceremonies. Not everyone who chooses Judaism will want such a ritual, but, when they are conducted with sensitivity and taste, the experience of many of my students has convinced me that they can be extremely powerful. I have received nothing but positive feedback from those congregations which have instituted such a public ceremony as part of the regular Shabbat service. The new Jews invariably experience an outpouring of love and affection. Congregants, not only become witnesses to the act of choosing Judaism, but are also reminded of the value, worth, and beauty of Judaism which made it attractive to someone not born a Jew. Some congregations, now more comfortable with public conversion ceremonies, also sponsor an Oneg Shabbat in honor of the newest member of the household of Israel.

6.   A one-year free temple membership.

Experience shows that a great percentage of Jews by choice fall away from Jewish life because they try to find their way in Judaism without the benefit of a community. I urge that every congregation make it a policy to extend one year's free congregational membership to any individual who is converted by the congregation's rabbi. But that's not enough!

7.   Create an adoptive-families program.

Immediately upon conversion, each Jew by choice and his or her family should be assigned a carefully screened adoptive family from among the active membership of the congregation. During the course of the first Jewish year, these adoptive families would make the newest member of the congregation aware of the many programs and services offered by the temple, would invite him or her to at least one Shabbat dinner at their home, would arrange for the new Jew to be contacted by various affiliates of the congregation, and, in general, would make him or her feel valued and welcomed as part of the synagogue community. After one year, the Jew by choice can then become an "adoptive family" for someone else. Thus, we create a two-year process of socialization into the Jewish community which will benefit the congregational member, the new Jew, and those who are touched by them both.

8.   Create post-conversion chavurot.

Jews by choice require substantial support during their first Jewish year. Accordingly, I urge the creation of a system of post-conversion chavurot within each congregation. These chavurot would be learning and discussion groups of limited duration, led by knowledgeable men and women who themselves chose Judaism, facilitating the study and experience of Judaism beyond that undertaken as part of the introduction to Judaism curriculum. In addition, though not a therapy group, such sessions would enable the frank and honest sharing of significant problems, doubts and anxieties, as well as possible solutions.

Seven Programs for Born-Jews

1. Use the temple bulletin for education and consciousness raising.

Very few temple bulletins are actively utilized to teach Judaism. If your temple bulletin does not function as an educational vehicle, I urge you to begin that process at once. In terms of Outreach, you might also consider bulletin dissemination of information on Judaism's stance on new Jews. The rabbi, educator, or new Jews themselves might prepare monthly articles on those aspects of our tradition which are directly applicable to this issue.

2. Programs for consciousness raising.

Conversion can easily become the theme of an Oneg Shabbat, a family camp weekend, or an adult education program. All too few Jews actually know Judaism's positive position vis-à-vis new Jews, and the inadvertent pain and confusion that Jewish bias and insensitivity often occasion. A program such as this can get those issues out into the open and serve to ameliorate them.

109

3. A bibliography of books and articles.

Especially since the advent of the UAHC's program of
Outreach, many Jews have expressed an interest in learning about Jewish attitudes toward conversion. You might
consider providing a bibliography of relevant books and
materials drawn from the list at the conclusion of this
book.

4. A Jewish bookstore for your temple.

Almost every congregation has a sisterhood gift shop.
What we need as much as that congregation's gift
shop, however, is a Jewish bookstore, stocked with texts
and materials on basic Judaism, both for Jews by choice
and born-Jews who wish to learn more about their heritage.

5. Support groups for Jewish parents.

Create/support discussion groups for Jewish parents
whose child has married, or is about to marry, a new
Jew. By doing so, the temple can provide them with
the same sort of insight and guidance that post-conversion groups offer to Jews by choice. A number of
congregations have begun to offer these groups. Par-
ticipating parents report that discussions have helped
to relieve their feelings of guilt and have helped them
to be supportive of their children without being—or
seeming—overly aggressive.

6. Courses for the religious school.

Sociologists tell us that, in the not too distant future, one out of every two Jewish marriages may include a partner not born in a Jewish home. Accordingly, I urge the inclusion of mini-courses or discussions on conversions at all levels of the religious school. It is often possible to have a knowledgeable Jew by choice visit the religious school and talk with the children, answering their questions. This also presents the students with a model of a man or woman who has chosen Judaism and who is familiar and close to them.

7. Books for the temple library.

Be sure to establish a basic Judaism bookshelf in your congregational library. In addition, be sure to display other Jewish books, records, and, if possible, a shelf of Jewish ritual objects for the home.

Each of the fifteen programs I have mentioned is doable —and doable now! You will be amazed at how much these simple efforts will enrich your congregational life. I urge you to undertake each and every one of them immediately, and hope that you will share your success stories as well as new ideas with me during the months to come.

Did you read that correctly? Did I ask you to write to me about *your* success stories? That's right. Because none of these programs will come to fruition unless *you* are prepared to take responsibility for implementing them.

If you are reading this book, I make the assumption that you care. So now I ask you to express that caring by offering your time and energy to your temple and to the Jewish people, stepping forward to work, together with your rabbi and with the leadership of your congregation, in reaching out to Jews by choice and—in the process— reaching out to the future of the Jewish people.

A Closing Word

WHEN all is said and done, this book is about "owning" Judaism. If reading it has made you feel that a little larger piece of Judaism belongs to you, then I am happy.

If you have come to Judaism as an adult, or are in the process of making that decision, I hope that you have found words with which to express some of your feelings. Also, I hope you've come to realize that hundreds, thousands, of others have had those exact feelings. You are not alone. The Jewish people needs you. With time, commitment, and learning, you will take your place in the Jewish community.

If you are the Jewish friend, spouse, fiancé, or parent-in-law of one who has come to Judaism, I am deeply grateful to you for caring enough to read this book. I hope that I have sensitized you to what is in the hearts of many men and women who choose to cast their lot with that of the Jewish people, who freely elect to share our destiny and our heritage. Your loved ones need your support and your Jewish literacy. Please don't let them down.

We have an opportunity to forge a rare and magnificent alliance today. Jewish tradition tells us: "The converts of a generation are the witnesses of, and to, the generation." Those who choose Judaism are witnesses to the beauty and value of Jewish tradition. They can see born-Jews as we cannot see ourselves. And they can give that vision of ourselves back to us.

Born-Jews have the security of having been born-in, but often do not have the new eyes to see what they were born into. We can help each other. We convert non-Jews to Judaism, but we must also convert born-Jews to Judaism—the joyous, positive, celebratory enrichment of life that Judaism embodies. We must create a community of Jewish learners, stressing the essentials, the doing, the spiritual fulfillment of living a Jewish life.

In the final analysis, you see, we are all Jews by choice. All those who choose to live a Jewish life are Jews by choice. It's just that some of us were born to Jewish parents.

Together, then, let us make that lifelong commitment to live and learn as Jews, to know the richness of our Jewish birthright.

Let the time come speedily, and may we, together, bring it to be, when all Jews can say, understand fully, and mean:

How fortunate are we,
How good is our portion.

A Short Glossary of
Some Basic Jewish Words

JUDAISM has its own vocabulary, with most of its value terms, holidays, and rituals expressed in Hebrew or Yiddish. The more terms you know, the more confident you'll feel.

What follows is a basic starter list of words and phrases you'll hear frequently. The list is not meant to be complete for it, too, is a beginning.

Do not be overwhelmed by this glossary. Use as much of it as you need. A confession—the food list includes mostly Ashkenazic foods. The whole world of Sephardic cooking awaits you! But, because most American Jews are of Ashkenazic background, I chose to begin there. That's where I started, too.

Synagogue Terms

Aliyah (from the Hebrew "to go up")	To have an aliyah is to recite the blessings before and after the Torah reading.

Aron Hakodesh (Hebrew)	The ark in which the Torah scrolls are kept.
Bimah (from the Hebrew "high place")	The platform at the front of the synagogue at which the rabbi and others stand during the services.
Chazan (Hebrew "cantor")	Trained professional singer who sings or chants the liturgy.
Daven (Yiddish)	To engage in prayer.
Haftarah (Hebrew)	A reading from the prophetic books of the Bible which follows the reading from the Torah in the synagogue on Sabbaths and festivals. Each Torah portion has its own haftarah portion.
Minyan (Hebrew "count")	Ten persons usually required to begin a Jewish service.
Ner Tamid (Hebrew)	Eternal Light. The light which is in front of the Aron Hakodesh and is always kept burning.
Oneg Shabbat (Hebrew "joy of the Sabbath")	Celebration after Shabbat services which includes refreshments and sometimes singing and/or Israeli dancing.
Sefer Torah	The Torah scroll, containing the Five Books of Moses and read each week at services. It is kept in the aron or ark at the front of the synagogue. It is adorned with a mantle and crowns and a breastplate.
Shul (Yiddish)	Another word for synagogue.
Siddur (from the Hebrew "order")	The prayer book which is used during services.
Talit (Hebrew;	Prayer shawl with ritual fringes

sometimes pronounced "talis" by Ashkenazic Jews) worn during Shabbat or morning services. In Orthodox and Conservative synagogues all men and boys above bar mitzvah age wear a talit. In Reform Judaism, the wearing of a talit is an option. In recent years, women have also begun to wear the talit.

Holiday Terms

Shabbat

Chalah	See food terms.
Hamotsi (from the Hebrew "bring forth")	The blessing over bread or any meal in which bread is eaten.
Havdalah (from the Hebrew "to divide")	A ritual which marks the end of Shabbat.
Kiddush (from the Hebrew "sanctify")	The prayer at the beginning of the Sabbath and Jewish holy days, which is recited or chanted over a cup of wine.

The High Holy Days: Rosh Hashanah and Yom Kippur

Kol Nidre (Aramaic "all vows")	The prayer which ushers in Yom Kippur. It is sung by the cantor. During this solemn prayer, the

Torah scrolls are removed from the ark and held before the congregation.

Leshanah Tovah Tikatevu — "May you be inscribed for a good year." Sometimes shortened to "Shanah Tovah" or, in Yiddish, "A Gut Yohr." A New Year greeting to family and friends.

Machzor — The special prayer book used for Rosh Hashanah and Yom Kippur.

Rosh Hashanah (Hebrew) — The Jewish New Year, literally "head of the year."

Selichot (Hebrew "sorry") — Special prayers said at night, communally, on the Saturday night preceding Rosh Hashanah.

Shofar — The ram's horn blown on Rosh Hashanah and Yom Kippur.

Teshuvah (from the Hebrew "turn") — The Hebrew word for "repentance." The days between Rosh Hashanah and Yom Kippur are called the ten days of teshuvah.

Yom Kippur — The Day of Atonement, a day of fasting, prayer, and reflection.

Sukot

Etrog (a citron) — Fragrant fruit. The lulav and etrog are the major symbols of Sukot.

Lulav — Palm branch with a holder containing myrtle and willow sprigs over which a blessing is recited and which is shaken during Sukot.

Sukah (Hebrew "booth") — A temporary structure built for this holiday to remind us of the flimsy structures in which the Israelites lived as they wandered for forty years in the desert.

Chanukah

Chanukah (from the Hebrew "to dedicate")	The festival of dedication, occurring on the 25th day of the Hebrew month of Kislev and lasting for eight days. It is a nonbiblical holiday which commemorates the victory of the Maccabees over the Syrians in 167 B.C.E. and the rededication of the Temple in Jerusalem.
Chanukah Gelt	Small gifts of money sometimes given to children on Chanukah.
Chanukiah, Menorah	A candelabrum with one branch for each night—eight lights—of Chanukah plus one extra light, the shamash, from which the other lights are lit.
Dreidel (Yiddish)	A small, four-sided top with the Hebrew letters nun, gimel, hei, and shin on each side. Used for a special Chanukah game.
Latke	See food terms.

Purim

Gragger	Noisemaker used to drown out the name of Haman each time it is read in the Megillah.

119

| Hamantashen | See food terms. |
| Megillah (Hebrew "scroll") | Usually refers to the Book of Esther which is read in the synagogue on Purim. (There are five megillot: Esther, Ruth, Lamentations, Ecclesiastes, and Song of Songs.) |

Pesach

Afikoman	Piece of matzah which is hidden, at the beginning of the seder, to be found by the children. Once found, it is distributed to all to signal the conclusion of the seder.
Chamets	See food terms.
Haggadah (from the Hebrew "to tell")	The book containing the narrative of Israel's slavery in Egypt and the deliverance from bondage to freedom. It is read aloud at the Passover seder.
Matzah	Unleavened bread—Comes in flat, thin, perforated sheets. It is a reminder of the bread which the Israelites ate when they hurriedly left Egypt.
Seder (Hebrew "order")	The festive meal which ushers in the festival of Passover during which the story of the Exodus from Egypt is dramatically retold; special symbols are displayed and songs sung.

Symbolic foods of the seder

These are placed on a plate in the center of the table.

Betsah	Roasted egg. A symbol of life.
Bowls of Salt Water	In which to dip the karpas and hard-boiled eggs. A reminder of the tears shed by our enslaved ancestors.
Charoset (sometimes pronounced "charoses")	Ground nuts and apples mixed with honey, wine, and cinnamon. Symbolizes the mortar between the bricks made by the Israelites in slavery.
Karpas	Greens, usually parsley, symbolizing spring.
Maror (Hebrew "bitter")	Bitter herbs, usually horseradish, symbolizing the bitterness of slavery.
Matzah	See above.
Zeroa	Roasted lamb shankbone symbolizing the Pesach sacrifice in the Temple in Jerusalem.

Some Jewish Food Terms

Blintz	Similar to a crepe, a thin pancake which is filled, usually with a cottage cheese mixture or fruit, and rolled. Often served with sour cream.

121

Borsht	1. Beet soup often served cold with sour cream and/or boiled potato.
	2. Cabbage and beef soup served hot.
Chalah	A braided loaf of white bread. The Sabbath bread. On Rosh Hashanah it is frequently baked in a circular shape, often with raisins.
Chamets	Food which is not permissible on Passover because it contains leavening or certain leavened grains.
Fleishig (Yiddish)	Foods prepared with meat products which, according to the dietary laws, may not be eaten with milk or foods prepared with milk.
Gefilte fish	Chopped fish, eggs, and onions mixed, shaped into balls (or sometimes into a loaf), poached in simmering stock, and served cold with horseradish. Frequently the first course of a Shabbat or holiday meal.
Halvah	Candy made of honey, ground sesame seeds, and sometimes pistachio nuts and/or chocolate. Sweet!
Hamantashen ("Haman's Pockets")	Triangular pockets of dough filled with poppy seeds, stewed dried fruits, or jam. Traditionally made and eaten on Purim.
Latke	A potato pancake, traditionally eaten on Chanukah. Delicious with applesauce or sour cream.

Kneidel (Yiddish; pl., kneidlach)	A matzah meal dumpling, usually added to chicken broth.
Kosher (from the Hebrew "fit," "proper")	The noun form is kashrut. Refers to something which is fit to eat, according to the Jewish dietary laws. Food which is not kosher is called "treif."
Kreplach	Triangular dumplings, similar to ravioli, filled, usually with meat, and usually served in soup.
Kugel	A pudding of noodles or potatoes. There are sweet kugels, "salty" kugels, potato kugels, fried kugels, and dairy kugels!
Milchig (Yiddish)	Dairy foods (containing milk or milk products) which according to the dietary laws may not be eaten with, or immediately after, meat.
Pareve (Yiddish)	Neither fleishig nor milchig but neutral according to dietary laws. For example, fish, fruit, and vegetables are pareve.

Some Life-Cycle Terms

Birth and Education

Bar/Bat Mitzvah	Public ceremony, usually at age 13, recognizing a Jewish child's attain-

123

	ment of an age at which meaningful Jewish observance is possible.
Berit Hachayim	The ceremony, which occurs on the eighth day after birth, celebrating the birth of a baby girl.
Berit Milah (often "bris")	The circumcision ceremony occurring on the eighth day after the birth of a Jewish boy.
Bubbie (Yiddish; savta is the Hebrew)	Grandma.
Confirmation	A public reaffirmation of a Jewish teenager's determination to live as a Jew. Usually in tenth grade on the holiday of Shavuot.
Consecration	Celebration of the beginning of a child's Jewish education. Usually in the synagogue during Sukot.
Kvater and Kvaterin	Godparents.
Mohel (from the Hebrew "circumcise")	The person who often performs the ritual circumcision, the berit milah, eight days after the birth of a male baby. In some cases a surgeon may co-officiate with a rabbi.
Sandak	The man who holds the baby during the circumcision. This is an honor which generally is accorded a relative or close friend.
Zeyde (Yiddish; sava is the Hebrew)	Grandfather.

124

A Short Glossary of Some Basic Jewish Words

Marriage and the Home

Chatan (Hebrew; sometimes pronounced "chasen")	Bridegroom.
Chaseneh (Yiddish)	Wedding.
Chupah	A wedding canopy under which the wedding ceremony takes place.
Get (Hebrew)	A religious divorce which terminates a Jewish marriage.
Kalah	A bride.
Ketubah (from the Hebrew "to write")	The Jewish marriage contract, often read during the wedding ceremony. Although there are standard, printed ketubot, you are free to design your own or have one made especially for you.
Kiddushin (from the Hebrew "holy")	The Jewish wedding ceremony, the marriage vows.
Mezuzah	A small container which is affixed, at a slant, to the right side of the front door of a Jewish home. Inside the mezuzah is a tiny rolled parchment or paper on which is printed verses from Deuteronomy 6:4–9 and 11:13–21.
Pushke (Yiddish)	A small can or special container kept in the house in which money is collected for charity. Many or-

ganizations provide their own pushkes. A wonderful custom to perpetuate is to drop some coins into the pushke before lighting Shabbat candles (see tsedakah).

Death

Alav Hashalom (masculine) Aleha Hashalom (feminine)	Literally, "On him/her peace"; roughly equivalent to the English, "May he/she rest in peace."
Mourner's Kaddish	An ancient prayer, in Aramaic, said at the end of all synagogue services, sanctifying God's name, recited by those who mourn. This prayer is recited at the graveside at the end of a funeral as well as on the anniversary of a death (yahrzeit).
Shivah (Hebrew "seven")	A period of seven days of mourning following the funeral during which the immediate family receives mourners at home. Shivah is not observed on Shabbat or certain other festivals.
Sheloshim (Hebrew "thirty")	The period of thirty days following a death during which the immediate family refrains from attending parties and other social events.
Yahrzeit (Yiddish; from the German "anniversary")	The anniversary of the death of a member of the family, observed on the Hebrew date of the death. There are special yahrzeit candles

which may be available in your market or in a store specializing in Jewish religious articles. A yahrzeit candle is a special candle in a glass container which burns for twenty-four hours. It is lit at sundown of the day previous to the anniversary. Frequently, the name of the person is also mentioned in the synagogue on the Shabbat of the yahrzeit.

Yizkor (from the Hebrew "remember")	Synagogue memorial service which occurs on Yom Kippur, Sukot, Pesach, and Shavuot.

Terms Relating to Jewish Texts

Bible	Also referred to as the TaNaCH. Consists of the Torah, the Prophets, and the Writings.
Gemara (from the Hebrew "finish")	Compilation of commentary on the Mishnah by scholars in Babylonia about the end of the fifth century.
Mishnah	The collection and codification of the "Oral Law" which was compiled around 160–200 C.E.
Talmud	The Mishnah and Gemara together.
Torah	The Five Books of Moses. Also, the scroll, kept in the ark, from which Jews read each week.

127

Some General Jewish Terms

Ashkenazic	Refers to the Jews who lived in Central and Eastern Europe. Many immigrated to America at the turn of the century and are the ancestors of the majority of North American Jews.
Chutspah	Nerve, effrontery, arrogance.
Galut (Hebrew; referred to as "Diaspora")	Exile—the dispersion of the Jews in lands beyond Israel.
Eretz Yisrael (Hebrew)	The Land of Israel.
Halachah (from the Hebrew word "to walk")	Orthodox Jewish law.
Hatikvah (Hebrew "The Hope")	The national anthem of the State of Israel.
Lechayim (Hebrew "to life")	A toast offered before drinking wine or liquor.
Mazal Tov	Literally, good luck; meaning "congratulations."
Mentsch (Yiddish)	A person who is honest, sensitive, decent, admirable.
Mitzvah (from the Hebrew "command")	(Divine) commandment; a good act or an ethical deed.
Rachmones (Yiddish; from the Hebrew "mercy")	Compassion, mercy.

Sephardic	Spanish and Portuguese Jews and their descendants as well as Jews from the Near East and North Africa.
Simchah	A happy occasion.
Tsedakah (from the Hebrew "righteous")	This term is most frequently translated as "charity," but there is actually no Hebrew word for "charity." Tsedakah really connotes establishing justice in the world through righteous and compassionate behavior.
Yarmulke (Yiddish; kipah is the Hebrew)	A skullcap worn by some Jews. It became customary for men to cover their heads as a sign of respect and reverence for God. Many traditional men cover their heads all the time. Others do so only while engaged in prayer, Jewish study, in home ritual, or at meals. For many modern Jews, including Reform Jews, covering the head is seen as an option rather than as a requirement.
Yom Tov (Hebrew "a good day," meaning "holiday"; sometimes "yuntif")	A holiday greeting. One general holiday greeting, derived from the Yiddish, is "Good (or 'Gut') Yuntif"—Happy Holiday!

"Make books your companions; let your bookshelves be your gardens: bask in their beauty, gather their fruit, pluck their roses, take their spices and myrrh. And, when your soul be weary, change from garden to garden, and from prospect to prospect."

JUDAH IBN TIBBON
twelfth century

Some Basic Jewish Books
for Your Home

JEWISH BOOKS are your surest door to a personal Jewish past and a literate Jewish future. Reading and study, if joined with experience, will make you more secure in your Jewishness and better able to touch the lives of others.

The bibliography which follows was compiled and annotated by Ronald S. Mass, a rabbinic student at the New York campus of the Hebrew Union College-Jewish Institute of Religion.

Ron prepared this list with the average Jew in mind, selecting those books which he and his colleagues felt would be the best introduction to a particular field.

Will you read all of the books listed? Probably not. We hope, however, that you make some of these books your close companions in your journey toward Jewish knowledge and identity.

American Jewish History and Culture

Glazer, Nathan. *American Judaism.* Revised edition. University of Chicago Press, 1972.

A historical survey of the Jewish religion in America. Traces the development, politics, and beliefs of the major Jewish religious groups and examines how the various movements have interacted with the dynamics of American life.

Anti-Semitism

Poliakov, Leon. *The History of Anti-Semitism.* Vol. 1: *From the Time of Christ to the Court Jews.* Translated from the French by Richard Howard. Schocken, 1974.

Poliakov, Leon. *The History of Anti-Semitism.* Vol. 2: *From Mohammed to the Marranos.* Translated from the French by Natalie Gerardi. Vanguard, 1974.

A classic study of the history and development of anti-Semitism.

Reuther, Rosemary. *Faith and Fratricide.* Seabury Press, 1974.

A brilliant study of the theological roots of anti-Semitism.

Archeology

Michener, James A. *The Source.* Fawcett, 1978.

A remarkable novel which skillfully recounts thousands of years of history in Israel through the wonders of archeology.

Yadin, Yigael. *Masada: Herod's Fortress and the Zealots' Last Stand.* Random House, 1966.

Elaborately illustrated volume about the Masada expedition. A step-by-step description of the excavation, as well as a history of Masada in light of the archeological evidence.

Yadin, Yigael. *The Message of the Scrolls.* Grosset & Dunlap, 1962.

Written for the general reader with an interest in the Bible, in the history of the Jewish people, and in Christianity. Seeks to answer many of the questions about the Dead Sea Scrolls, their discovery, their content, and their religious, social, and historical significance. Illustrated.

Art, Music, and Dance

Eisenstein, Judith Kaplan. *Heritage of Jewish Music: The Music of the Jewish People.* Union of American Hebrew Congregations, 1972.

With more than 100 musical examples from Jewry's cultural treasure house, this rich and varied collection illustrates how the music has grown out of the Jewish experience and how it reflects Jewish values through the ages and around the world.

Freelander, Daniel H., ed. *Songs NFTY Sings.* Union of American Hebrew Congregations, 1980.

Two hundred and fifteen popular Hebrew songs, prayers, and worship responses, complete with Hebrew text, English translations, and transliterations. Includes old favorites like "Yerushalayim shel Zahav," "Shalom Rav," "Mayim," "Lach Yerushalayim," and many more.

Kampf, Avram. *Contemporary Synagogue Art: Developments in the United States, 1945–1965.* Union of American Hebrew Congregations, 1976.

Lovely work which offers the reader a rich insight into the various art forms that go into making the modern synagogue a place of worship and beauty.

Roth, Cecil. *Jewish Art: An Illustrated History.* New York Graphic Society, 1971.

Four hundred and fifty lavish illustrations and twelve colorplates combine to give this book a regal touch. A complete history of Jewish art ranging from the second millennium B.C.E. to the present day.

Smolover, Raymond, and Stern, Malcolm, eds. *Songs and Hymns for Gates of Prayer.* American Conference of Cantors and Central Conference of American Rabbis, 1977.

Every song in *Gates of Prayer*—full text, transliteration, melody and chording for guitar or piano accompaniment.

Atlases and Travel Guides

Postal, Bernard, and Koppman, Lionel. *American Jewish Landmarks: A Travel Guide and History.* Vol. 1. Fleet Press, 1977.

State-by-state, city-by-city record of Jewish landmarks, institutions, agencies, museums, libraries, etc. Each state is introduced by a short history of the Jews in the area. An impressive catalog of information about the American Jewish community.

Postal, Bernard, and Koppman, Lionel. *American Jewish Landmarks: A Travel Guide and History, the South and Southwest.* Vol. 2. Fleet Press, 1979.

Postal, Bernard, and Koppman, Lionel. *Jewish Landmarks of New York: A Travel Guide and History.* Fleet Press, 1978.

A remarkable document. Informative history of New York's Jewish community plus detailed listings of Jewish museums, restaurants, libraries, shops, federated agencies, synagogues, cemeteries, and sites and shrines. More than a manual for sightseers.

Vilnay, Zev. *The Guide to Israel.* Twentieth revised edition. International Publications Service, 1978.

The best guide for those wishing to experience the rich cultural and historical fabric of Israel.

Attitudes and Concepts

Efron, Benjamin, and Rubin, Alvan D. *Coming of Age: Your Bar/Bat Mitzvah*. Union of American Hebrew Congregations, 1977.
 Completely revised, popular orientation manual for bar/bat mitzvah candidates and their parents.

Feldman, David M. *Marital Relations, Birth Control, and Abortion in Jewish Law*. Schocken, 1974.
 Traditional Jewish perspective on marital relations, contraception, and abortion. The author examines these issues through the teachings of the Talmud, codes, commentaries, and rabbinic responsa.

Gittelsohn, Roland B. *Love, Sex, and Marriage: A Jewish View*. Union of American Hebrew Congregations, 1980.
 A modern, candid discussion of Jewish sexual ethics for grade eleven and up.

Goodman, Philip, and Goodman, Hanna, eds. *The Jewish Marriage Anthology*. Jewish Publication Society, 1965.
 A volume of ancient and modern sources that depict the unique Jewish understanding of marriage.

Lamm, Maurice. *The Jewish Way in Love and Marriage*. Harper and Row, 1980.
 A popular and authoritative presentation of Jewish teaching on love and marriage in light of the traditions and laws of the Bible and of its interpreters throughout the ages.

Riemer, Jack, ed. *Jewish Reflections on Death*. Schocken, 1976.
 Sensitively chosen collection of essays that portray the historical development and current status of the Jewish way of death.

Seltzer, Sanford. *Jews and Non-Jews: Falling in Love*. Union of American Hebrew Congregations, 1976.
 An informal guide to interfaith marriage for the couples, their families, and the rabbis who counsel them.

Silver, Abba H. *Where Judaism Differed*. Macmillan, 1956.
 A lively account of the distinctive values and outlook of Judaism and an exploration of the sharp divergencies between Judaism and Christianity.

Basic Judaism

Bial, Morrison D. *Liberal Judaism at Home: The Practices of Modern Reform Judaism*. Revised edition. Union of American Hebrew Congregations, 1971.
 A personal, well-organized guide to Reform religious practice.

Maslin, Simeon J., ed. *Gates of Mitzvah*. Central Conference of American Rabbis, 1979.
 A guide to Jewish observance, throughout the life cycle, from the Reform point of view. Includes sections on birth, childhood, education, marriage, the

Some Basic Jewish Books for Your Home

Jewish home, tsedakah, death and mourning, and kashrut. Also contains notes and references for further study.

Schauss, Hayyim. *The Lifetime of a Jew: Throughout the Ages of Jewish History.* Union of American Hebrew Congregations, 1976.

The rites, ceremonies, and folklore that have attended the life of a Jew.

Steinberg, Milton. *Basic Judaism.* Harcourt Brace Jovanovich, 1947.

A succinct, lucid discussion of the fundamentals of Judaism.

Syme, Daniel B. *The Jewish Home.* Union of American Hebrew Congregations. Published periodically.

Insightfully written, illustrated pamphlets highlighting the why and how of Jewish living in the home. Included in this ongoing series are descriptions of Shabbat, the Jewish festivals, life-cycle ceremonies, and Jewish symbols.

Bible

The Book of Psalms: A New Translation According to the Traditional Hebrew Text. Jewish Publication Society, 1972.

This contemporary translation casts new light on one of the most important books of the Bible, giving the reader new insights into the ancient text.

The Five Megilloth and the Book of Jonah. Jewish Publication Society, 1969.

Strikingly illustrated, modern translations of the books of Song of Songs, Ruth, Lamentations, Ecclesiastes, Esther, and Jonah, prepared under the editorship of Professor H. L. Ginsberg.

Freehof, Solomon B. *Preface to Scripture: A Guide to the Understanding of the Bible in Accordance with the Jewish Tradition.* Behrman House, 1950.

Popular introduction to the Jewish Bible for the layperson. Discusses such topics as the structure and canonization of Scripture, the place of the Bible in worship, the importance of modern biblical criticism and archeology in exploring the text, and the Bible as literature. Contains an extensive section of excerpts from Scripture in English.

Orlinsky, Harry M. *Understanding the Bible through History and Archeology.* Ktav, 1969.

Coherent account of the society that produced the Bible. The author makes clear how Jewish religious concepts developed in the context of actual historical situations. He sheds light on the basis of the relationship between the Israelites and God, the fundamental concept of justice, and the unique worth of the individual which the prophets preached.

The Prophets, Nevi'im: A New Translation of the Holy Scriptures According to the Traditional Hebrew Text. Jewish Publication Society, 1978.

A new English translation of the major and minor prophets rendered in an accurate, fluent, and idiomatic fashion.

Samuel, Maurice. *Certain People of the Book.* Union of American Hebrew Congregations, 1977.

Timeless, witty, intimate portraits of biblical figures.

135

Sandmel, Samuel. *The Enjoyment of Scripture: The Law, the Prophets, and the Writings.* Oxford University Press, 1974.

Concerned with the literary method and quality of the various kinds of writings found in the Tanach.

The Torah: The Five Books of Moses. Jewish Publication Society, 1962.

A scholarly but readable English translation of the Pentateuch taking into account the latest linguistic researches and archeological discoveries.

The Torah: A Modern Commentary. Union of American Hebrew Congregations, 1981.

This first major Reform commentary on the Five Books of Moses contains the Hebrew text, the new translation by the Jewish Publication Society, incisive commentary, and related writings from an encyclopedic range of sources. Also included are the haftarot for each sidrah and for special days.

Plaut, W. Gunther. Commentaries on *Genesis, Exodus, Numbers,* and *Deuteronomy.*

Bamberger, Bernard J. Commentary on *Leviticus.*

Chasidism

Buber, Martin. *The Legend of the Baal-Shem.* Schocken, 1969.

The major concepts of chasidic life followed by twenty stories about the life of the Baal Shem, the founder of the chasidic movement.

Buber, Martin. *Tales of the Hasidim.* 2 volumes. Schocken, 1961.

The classic collections of the legends of the *"tsadikim,"* the righteous masters of the Chasidim.

Newman, Louis I., ed. *The Hasidic Anthology: Tales and Teachings of the Hasidim.* Schocken, 1963.

Tales, proverbs, and paradoxes through which the chasidic masters conveyed their wisdom to their disciples, along with an introduction providing a guide to the history of Chasidism.

Wiesel, Elie. *Souls on Fire: Portraits and Legends of Hasidic Masters.* Random House, 1973.

Delightful retelling of the tales of the chasidic masters of the eighteenth and nineteenth centuries. Includes portraits of Israel Baal Shem Tov, Levi-Yitzhak of Berditchev, and Nachman of Bratzlav.

Christianity and Judaism

Sandmel, Samuel. *A Jewish Understanding of the New Testament.* Ktav, 1974.

A description of the New Testament as seen through the eyes of a prominent Jewish scholar. Contains sections on Paul, the Synoptic Gospels, and other writings.

Sandmel, Samuel. *We Jews and Jesus.* Oxford University Press, 1973.

Written in a nontechnical style for the layperson, this book describes the what and why of the Jewish attitude to Jesus.

136

Some Basic Jewish Books for Your Home

Weiss-Rosmarin, Trude. *Judaism and Christianity: The Differences.* Jonathan David, 1965.

Concise, popular presentation of the teachings of and differences between Judaism and Christianity.

Eastern European Life, Literature, and Culture

Dawidowicz, Lucy S., ed. *The Golden Tradition.* Holt, Rinehart and Winston, 1967.

A rich collection of essays and documents depicting the vibrant world of Eastern European Jewry from the end of the eighteenth century until its cataclysmic destruction in World War II. Contains sections on Chasidism, education, Zionism, the arts, and politics, as well as a lengthy historical introduction.

Samuel, Maurice. *The World of Sholom Aleichem.* Knopf, 1943.

A pilgrimage through Sholom Aleichem's world, visiting the townlets and villages of the famous Pale of Settlement, recounting the adventures of the chief characters in the works of Sholom Aleichem, and re-creating the folklore, the outlook, and the memories that were in part transplanted to America.

Zborowski, Mark, and Herzog, Elizabeth. *Life Is with People: The Culture of the Shtetl.* Schocken, 1962.

Anthropological study of the world of Eastern European Jewry dealing with, among other things, the Sabbath, tsedakah, marriage, and the Jewish home.

Family

Bial, Morrison D. *Your Jewish Child.* Union of American Hebrew Congregations, 1978.

A primer to help parents and parents-to-be create a Jewish home that promotes Jewish identity. Topics covered include simple ritual, baby-naming, prayer, and how to tell your children about God, death, and afterlife.

Food

Levi, Shonie B., and Kaplan, Sylvia R. *Guide for the Jewish Homemaker.* Schocken, 1965.

Practical counsel in such matters as developing menus, planning a wedding, and celebrating holidays and customs with special recipes.

Nathan, Joan. *The Jewish Holiday Kitchen.* Schocken, 1979.

A presentation of the history, food requirements, and traditions of each of the Jewish holidays along with a collection of recipes.

Rockland, Mae S. *The Jewish Party Book: A Contemporary Guide to Customs, Crafts, and Foods.* Schocken, 1979.

Hundreds of recipes, music, and crafts projects for gifts and decorations for every kind of Jewish celebration.

Hebrew

Adler, L. W., and Castberg, C. *Reading Hebrew: A Programmed Instruction Book.* Behrman House, 1972.

A step-by-step programmed method for the teaching of Hebrew at school or at home. Flash cards, drill book, and teacher's guide are also available.

Samuel, Edith. *Your Jewish Lexicon.* Union of American Hebrew Congregations. (To be published early in 1982.)

Series of short articles discussing basic Hebrew terms and phrases and the values and concepts they express. In English, Hebrew, and English transliteration.

Shumsky, Abraham, and Shumsky, Adaia. *Alef-Bet: A Hebrew Primer.* Union of American Hebrew Congregations, 1980.

An entirely phonetic approach to the learning of Hebrew. Completion of *Alef-Bet* equips students with the basic skills for reading the siddur and the berachot while developing a knowledge of Judaism. Designed for children, but helpful to adults as well.

History

Bamberger, Bernard J. *The Story of Judaism.* Schocken, 1964.

Over 3,000 years of Jewish existence distilled into a single readable volume.

Eisenberg, Azriel; Goodman, Hannah Grad; and Kass, Alvin. *Eyewitnesses to Jewish History: From 586 B.C.E. to 1967.* Union of American Hebrew Congregations, 1972.

Collection of first-hand reports by people who themselves lived through major events in Jewish history. Some of the events "witnessed" include the revolt of the Maccabees, the Spanish Inquisition, the uprising in the Warsaw Ghetto, and the capture of Eichmann.

Roth, Cecil. *A History of the Jews: From Earliest Times through the Six Day War.* Revised edition. Schocken, 1970.

Popular history tracing the social, religious, and cultural development of the Jewish people from the biblical era down to the present.

Sachar, Abram L. *History of the Jews.* Knopf, 1967.

A complete history of thirty centuries of Judaism, in which due emphasis is given to the economic, social, and environmental factors, as well as to religious and philosophical development.

138

Some Basic Jewish Books for Your Home

Sachar, Howard M. *The Course of Modern Jewish History*. Dell, 1977.
 Comprehensive and scholarly account of the Jews from the French Revolution to the present day. Depicts the social and cultural influences—both Jewish and non-Jewish—that have formed the civilization of Jews throughout the world.
Seltzer, Robert M. *Jewish People, Jewish Thought: The Jewish Experience in History*. Macmillan, 1980.
 Comprehensive one-volume overview of the Jewish people's social and political history set against the intellectual, religious, and cultural currents of the times and places in which Jews lived. An ambitious work, complete with maps, illustrations, and photographs.

Holidays, Festivals, and the Sabbath

Agnon, Shmuel Y. *The Days of Awe*. Schocken, 1965.
 Agnon's classic anthology of Jewish wisdom, skillfully crafted as a literary tone poem on the High Holy Days.
Bearman, Jane. *The Eight Nights: A Chanukah Counting Book*. Union of American Hebrew Congregations, 1979.
 A lively rhyme for each of the eight nights and exquisite full-color graphics present all the delights of Chanukah—lighting candles, singing songs, playing dreidel, eating latkes, and giving and receiving presents. An imaginative activity book for the very young.
Cashman, Greer Fay. *Jewish Days and Holidays*. SBS Publishing, Inc., 1979.
 A lavishly illustrated book for children depicting the joy and celebration of the Jewish holidays.
Gaster, Theodor H. *Festivals of the Jewish Year*. Peter Smith, 1962.
 The origins, rituals, customs, and contemporary meaning of the Jewish festivals, fasts, and holy days.
Goodman, Philip, ed. *The Hanukkah Anthology*. Jewish Publication Society, 1976.
 The seven holiday anthologies edited by Philip Goodman are useful guides for the meaningful celebration of the Jewish festivals. Each volume contains sections on the history of the holiday and its observance, the representation of the day in art, poetry and prose readings from both the ancient and modern sources, and the music associated with the celebration.
Goodman, Philip, ed. *The Passover Anthology*. Jewish Publication Society, 1961.
Goodman, Philip, ed. *The Purim Anthology*. Jewish Publication Society, 1949.
Goodman, Philip, ed. *The Rosh Hashanah Anthology*. Jewish Publication Society, 1970.
Goodman, Philip, ed. *The Shavuot Anthology*. Jewish Publication Society, 1975.
Goodman, Philip, ed. *The Sukkot and Simhat Torah Anthology*. Jewish Publication Society, 1973.
Goodman, Philip, ed. *The Yom Kippur Anthology*. Jewish Publication Society, 1971.

Heschel, Abraham J. *The Sabbath.* Farrar, Straus, and Giroux, 1975.

The author's magical celebration of the Sabbath and the sanctification of time over space.

Marcus, Audrey F., and Zwerin, Raymond A. *Shabbat Can Be.* Union of American Hebrew Congregations, 1979.

The warm feelings and images of Shabbat familiar to a small child are evoked in the simple text and lovely illustrations. For ages six to eight.

Marcus, Audrey F., and Zwerin, Raymond A. *But This Night Is Different.* Union of American Hebrew Congregations, 1981.

A beautiful and sensitive portrayal of Passover. For ages six to eight.

Schauss, Hayyim. *The Jewish Festivals: History and Observance.* Schocken, 1973.

Details the colorful story of the Jewish festivals and their development, their origin and background, their rich symbolism, ritual practices, and use of ceremonial objects.

A Shabbat Manual. Central Conference of American Rabbis, 1972.

A practical guide to the observance of Shabbat, including home services, Shabbat songs, selected readings, and a catalog of the weekly Torah and haftarah portions. A tape of blessings and Shabbat songs can be ordered with the manual.

Holocaust

Dawidowicz, Lucy S. *The War Against the Jews: 1933–1945.* Bantam, 1976.

A major study of the Holocaust. Intensively researched, comprehensive, and authoritative.

Dawidowicz, Lucy S. *A Holocaust Reader.* Behrman House, 1976.

The source documents upon which the author's *The War Against the Jews: 1933–1945* is based. Annotated with an introduction on how the documents were screened and authenticated.

Epstein, Helen. *Children of the Holocaust: Conversations with Sons and Daughters of Survivors.* Putnam, 1979.

Stories of children of survivors of the Nazi Holocaust and their private struggle to come to terms with their parents' past.

Frank, Anne. *Anne Frank: The Diary of a Young Girl.* Revised edition. Doubleday, 1967.

The remarkable, timeless diary of a young girl, describing the changes wrought upon eight people hiding out from the Nazis for two years during the occupation of Holland.

Friedlander, Albert H., ed. *Out of the Whirlwind: A Reader of Holocaust Literature.* Schocken, 1976.

A thorough and fascinating collection of writings, music, and art about the Holocaust. Includes selections by Elie Wiesel, Anne Frank, Leo Baeck, and Abraham J. Heschel.

Goldstein, Jacob; Knox, Israel; and Margoshes, Samuel. *Anthology of Holocaust Literature.* Atheneum, 1972.

An extensive collection of writings of and about the Holocaust. English translation of some of the most memorable works originally rendered in Yiddish, Hebrew, French, German, Russian, and Polish.

Hausner, Gideon. *Justice in Jerusalem.* Schocken, 1978.

Wrenching account of the Eichmann trial—the intense effort that went into the prosecution's preparation of the case and the grueling attempt to be fair while partisan in judging and convicting the man.

Hersey, John. *The Wall.* Modern Library, 1967.

A powerful work of historical fiction written in diary form about life in the Warsaw Ghetto during the Nazi occupation.

Morse, Arthur D. *While Six Million Died: Chronicle of American Apathy.* Hart, 1975.

The author builds a convincing case of US governmental indifference and national apathy in the face of the Holocaust. A significant and powerful report.

Pisar, Samuel. *Of Blood and Hope.* Little, Brown and Company, 1980.

Rabinowitz, Dorothy. *New Lives: Survivors of the Holocaust Living in America.* Avon, 1977.

The survivors themselves tell of individual reactions to liberation, to arrival in America, to starting new jobs and homes and families, and to finding their place in a world that did not understand the nightmare from which they had emerged.

Schwarz-Bart, André. *The Last of the Just.* Translated from the French by Stephen Becker. Bantam, 1973.

Memorable novel about the Holocaust, using the theme of the thirty-six just souls by whose merit the world continues to exist.

Spiritual Resistance: Art from Concentration Camps, 1940–1945. Union of American Hebrew Congregations, 1981.

A selection of drawings and paintings from the collection of Kibbutz Lohamei Haghetaot, Israel. Includes essays by Miriam Novitch, Lucy S. Dawidowicz, and Tom L. Freudenheim.

Suhl, Yuri, ed. and trans. *They Fought Back: The Story of the Jewish Resistance in Nazi Europe.* Schocken, 1975.

The story of Jewish resistance groups during the Holocaust—how they existed in almost every ghetto and concentration camp, active in sabotage, and in many cases carrying out successful armed revolts.

Volavkova, Hana, ed. *I Never Saw Another Butterfly: Children's Drawings and Poems from Terezin Concentration Camp, 1942–1944.* Translated from the Czech by Jeanne Nemcova. Schocken, 1978.

Unforgettable collection of drawings and poems by children in the Terezin concentration camp. The art survived; the children did not.

Wiesel, Elie. *Night.* Avon, 1972.

Powerful, autobiographical account of a young boy's experiences during the Holocaust.

141

Israel

Facts About Israel. Edited by Hanan Sher, in association with Moshe Aumann and Channa Palti. Israel Information Center, P.O. Box 13010, Jerusalem, 1977. Published periodically.

Rich compendium of facts about the modern State of Israel, including sections on history, geography, government, education, economy, foreign policy, and immigration.

Sachar, Howard M. *A History of Israel: From the Rise of Zionism to Our Time.* Knopf, 1979.

Best one-volume history of the modern State of Israel. Meticulously researched and intelligently written.

Law

Freehof, Solomon B. *Current Reform Responsa.* Ktav, 1969.

Responses to questions concerning the observance and interpretation of traditional Jewish customs and religious law by Dr. Freehof, a leading scholar in Reform Judaism.

Freehof, Solomon B. *Modern Reform Responsa.* Ktav, 1971.

Freehof, Solomon B. *Reform Responsa and Recent Reform Responsa.* Ktav, 1973.

Freehof, Solomon B. *The Responsa Literature and a Treasury of Responsa.* Ktav, 1973.

Jacobs, Louis. *Jewish Law.* Behrman House, 1968.

A young people's introduction to Halachah by a distinguished Jewish scholar. Includes selections from the traditional basic sources—halachic midrashim, Mishnah, Talmud, codes, and responsa.

Literature: Anthologies

Alter, Robert, ed. *Modern Hebrew Literature.* Behrman House, 1975.

The rebirth of creative writing in the Hebrew language—translated into English for the layperson and student alike—with selections from the works of the modern masters, from Mendele Mocher Sforim, Peretz, and Bialik to the flowering of today's Israeli writers: Oz, Yehoshua, and Amichai.

Anderson, Elliott. *Contemporary Israeli Literature.* Jewish Publication Society, 1977.

A comprehensive survey of Israeli writing since 1948. Includes work by established literary figures as well as by less-familiar names. Over thirty writers are represented in this collection.

Bellow, Saul, ed. *Great Jewish Short Stories.* Dell, 1963.

Representative selections from the short stories of the most prominent

Jewish authors of the last century. Includes writings of Agnon, Bellow, Singer, Babel, Peretz, and others.

Glatzer, Nahum N., ed. *A Jewish Reader: In Time and Eternity.* Schocken, 1961.

A sourcebook of postbiblical Jewish literature, spanning eighteen centuries of Jewish life and thought. The selections range over many fields: formal theology and simple faith, philosophy and folklore, practical law and mystical contemplation.

Howe, Irving, and Greenberg, Eliezer, eds. *A Treasury of Yiddish Poetry.* Schocken, 1976.

Exensive anthology of Yiddish poetry, reflecting the developments in Jewish life in the nineteenth and twentieth centuries and mirroring the literary techniques of the larger culture in which the poets lived.

Howe, Irving, and Greenberg, Eliezer, eds. *A Treasury of Yiddish Stories.* Schocken, 1973.

Selections from the works of the great masters of Yiddish prose form with an extensive introduction by the editors.

Leviant, Curt. *Masterpieces of Hebrew Literature: A Treasury of Two Thousand Years of Jewish Creativity.* Ktav, 1969.

A potpourri of two thousand years of postbiblical creativity, covering the major periods from the Apocrypha to the eighteenth century and presenting substantial selections of the important genres. Brief introductions are provided to place the author and his work in proper perspective.

Mintz, Ruth F. *Modern Hebrew Poetry: A Bilingual Anthology.* University of California Press, 1966.

One hundred and fifteen poems representing the styles and themes of twenty-eight of the important Hebrew poets of this century. Includes selections from the poetry of Bialik, Tschernikhovski, Shlonsky, Alterman, Goldberg, Bluwstein, and Amichai.

Schwarz, Leo W., ed. *The Jewish Caravan: Great Stories of Twenty-five Centuries.* Schocken, 1976.

Vast selection of Jewish writing, both ancient and modern. Includes such literary giants as S. Y. Agnon, Sholom Aleichem, Franz Kafka, I. B. Singer, and Isaac Babel.

Liturgy

Bronstein, Herbert, ed. *A Passover Haggadah.* Central Conference of American Rabbis, 1974.

New haggadah of the Reform movement. Contains twenty original watercolors, the complete Passover home service, and an extensive song section musically annotated.

Glatzer, Nahum N., ed. *Language of Faith: A Selection from the Most Expressive Jewish Prayers.* Schocken, 1974.

Prayers from ancient and modern times on such subjects as the Creation, the presence of God, thanksgiving, the cycle of life, Sabbath, and peace.

143

Hoffman, Lawrence, ed. *Gates of Understanding.* Union of American Hebrew Congregations, 1977.

Companion volume to *Gates of Prayer,* giving sources for all of the prayers, meditations, and songs. Chapters on the language and origin of prayer, the Reform liturgy, music in Jewish worship, the role of God, and the structure of the prayer book.

Millgram, Abraham E. *Jewish Workshop.* Jewish Publication Society, 1971.

Surveys the origins, development, and contemporary significance of Jewish liturgy. The author explains all major aspects of Jewish worship and discusses related theological issues as well.

Petuchowski, Jakob J., ed. *Understanding Jewish Prayer.* Ktav, 1972.

The first part deals with the dynamics of Jewish worship from the biblical period through modern times. It discusses such problems as the concept of prayer as "obligation," the place of the Hebrew language in Jewish worship, and the modern challenges to prayer. The second half of the book consists of an anthology of essays on Jewish prayer contributed by outstanding Jewish scholars.

Stern, Chaim, ed. *Gates of the House.* Central Conference of American Rabbis, 1977.

Home prayer book containing services for special occasions in life and scores of meditations for Shabbat, festivals, and other traditional occasions.

Stern, Chaim, ed. *Gates of Prayer: The New Union Prayerbook.* Central Conference of American Rabbis, 1975.

Standard liturgical work of the Reform movement. Contains services for weekdays, Sabbaths, and festivals, as well as for Israel Independence Day, Holocaust Remembrance Day, and Tishah Be'av. Also contains special readings, meditations, and forty pages of songs complete with transliterations.

Stern, Chaim, ed. *Gates of Repentance.* Central Conference of American Rabbis, 1978.

Prayer book of the Reform movement for the Days of Awe. Contains services, readings, meditations, and songs for Rosh Hashanah and Yom Kippur. Companion volume to *Gates of Prayer.*

Medieval Jewish Philosophy

Guttman, Julius. *Philosophies of Judaism: The History of Jewish Philosophy from Biblical Times to Franz Rosenzweig.* Schocken, 1973.

Authoritative history of Jewish philosophy, from biblical times through its period of great vitality in the Middle Ages to the turn of this century.

Modern Jewish Thought

Borowitz, Eugene B. *Modern Varieties of Jewish Thought: A Presentation and Interpretation.* Behrman House, 1981.

A thoughtful presentation and analysis of the philosophies of the major Jewish thinkers of our time. Includes chapters on Hermann Cohen, Leo Baeck, Mordecai Kaplan, Franz Rosenzweig, Martin Buber, Abraham Heschel, and Joseph D. Soleveitchik.

Buber, Martin. *I and Thou.* Translated by Walter Kaufman. Scribner, 1970.

The philosopher's magnum opus, translated and with notes by Walter Kaufman.

Glatzer, Nahum N., ed. *Modern Jewish Thought: A Source Reader.* Schocken, 1976.

Selections from the writings of the most important modern Jewish thinkers, surveying the major intellectual concerns of Jews from the period of Moses Mendelssohn until today. Each section is preceded by a brief introduction.

Heschel, Abraham J. *God in Search of Man: A Philosophy of Judaism.* Farrar, Straus, and Giroux, 1976.

A spellbinding, powerful work by one of the towering figures of contemporary Judaism.

Heschel, Abraham J. *Man Is Not Alone: A Philosophy of Religion.* Farrar, Straus, and Giroux, 1975.

A companion volume to *God in Search of Man.* A discussion of the principles of faith and the challenge to modern man to understand himself and the world about him.

Rosenzweig, Franz. *Star of Redemption.* Translated by William W. Hallo. Beacon Press, 1972.

One of the most significant contributions to Jewish theology in the twentieth century. A key document of modern existential thought.

Seltzer, Robert M. *Jewish People, Jewish Thought: The Jewish Experience in History.* Macmillan, 1980.

Comprehensive one-volume overview of the Jewish people's social and political history set against the intellectual, religious, and cultural currents of the times and places in which Jews lived. An ambitious work, tracing the evolution of Jewish thought through the centuries, complete with maps, illustrations, and photographs.

Mysticism

Kushner, Lawrence. *Honey from the Rock: 10 Gates of Jewish Mysticism.* Harper and Row, 1977.

Autobiographical tales, age-old Jewish legends, and biblical quotations poetically usher the reader through the ten gates of mystical experience, from the wilderness of preparation, through learning to recognize messengers of the Most High, to the ultimate union with the Creator.

Weiner, Herbert. *Nine and a Half Mystics: The Kabbala Today.* Macmillan, 1971.

A treasure hunt for the life secrets of the mystical tradition known as the Kabbalah. The author introduces us to contemporary representatives of this tradition who are challenged to relate their hidden wisdom to problems of our day.

Periodicals

Commentary (1945). 165 East 56th Street, New York, New York 10022. Norman Podhoretz. Monthly. American Jewish Committee.

Congress bi-Monthly (1934). 15 East 84th Street, New York, New York 10028. Herbert Poster. Monthly (except July and August). American Jewish Congress.

Hadassah Magazine (1921). 50 West 58th Street, New York, New York 10019. Jesse Zel Lurie. Monthly (except June–July and August–September). Hadassah Women's Zionist Organization of America.

The Jerusalem Post (International Edition). 110 East 59th Street, New York, New York 10022. Weekly.

The Jewish Spectator (1935). P.O. Box 2016, Santa Monica, California 90406. Trude Weiss-Rosmarin. Quarterly.

Journal of Reform Judaism. 790 Madison Avenue, New York, New York 10021. Bernard Martin. Quarterly. Central Conference of American Rabbis.

Judaism (1952). 15 East 84th Street, New York, New York 10028. Robert Gordis. Quarterly. American Jewish Congress.

Keeping Posted. 838 Fifth Avenue, New York, New York 10021. Aron Hirt-Manheimer. Leader's Edition available. Magazines also available as mini-courses. Union of American Hebrew Congregations.

Lilith (1976). 250 West 57th Street, New York, New York 10019. Susan Weidman Schneider. Quarterly.

Midstream (1955). 515 Park Avenue, New York, New York 10022. Joel Carmichael. Monthly. Theodor Herzl Foundation.

Moment (1975). 55 Chapel Street, Newton, Massachusetts 02160. Leonard Fein. Monthly (except January–February, July–August).

Near East Report (1957). 444 North Capitol Street, N.W., Washington, D.C. 20001. Alan M. Tigay. Weekly. Near East Research, Inc.

Present Tense (1973). 165 East 56th Street, New York, New York 10022. Murray Polner. Quarterly. American Jewish Committee.

Reform Judaism (1972). 838 Fifth Avenue, New York, New York 10021. Aron Hirt-Manheimer. Newspaper distributed free to congregations but also available at a low subscription rate. Union of American Hebrew Congregations.

Sh'ma (1970). Box 567, Port Washington, New York 11050. Eugene B. Borowitz. Biweekly (except June, July, August).

Rabbinic Judaism

Cohen, Abraham. *Everyman's Talmud.* Schocken, 1975.
    An explanation of the Talmud's history and makeup is followed by summaries of the major teachings by subject.

Some Basic Jewish Books for Your Home

Ginzberg, Louis. *Legends of the Jews.* 7 volumes. Jewish Publication Society, 1956.
  Monumental, seven-volume classic on Jewish folklore. Brings together the principal biblical legends, culled from a wide variety of literary sources. One-volume abridgement is also available.

Glatzer, Nahum N., ed. *Hammer on the Rock: A Midrash Reader.* Schocken, 1962.
  A masterful selection of over 200 representative passages from the Talmud and Midrash.

Hertz, Joseph H. *Pirke Aboth: Sayings of the Fathers.* Behrman House, 1945.
  The complete Hebrew text with a lucid English translation and notes by the former chief rabbi of the British Empire.

Montefiore, C. G., and Loewe, H., eds. *A Rabbinic Anthology.* Schocken, 1970.
  A vast compendium of passages of talmudic and midrashic literature. Useful for scholar and layperson alike.

Neusner, Jacob. *Invitation to the Talmud.* Harper and Row, 1976.
  Superb introduction to the Talmud and the rabbinic world for the beginning student. Chapter headings include "The Mishnah," "The Tosefta," "The Babylonian Talmud," and "The Palestinian Talmud."

Steinsaltz, Adin. *The Essential Talmud.* Translated from the Hebrew by Chaya Galai. Bantam, 1977.
  Summarizes the history, structure, content, method, and main principles of the Talmud in simple, concise language. Suitable both for the enlightened reader as well as for those who are coming to the Talmud for the first time.

Recordings

Songs NFTY Sings:
  No. 2: Shiru Shir Chadash
  No. 3: Ten Shabbat V'Ten Shalom
  No. 4: The Time of Singing
  No. 5: NFTY at 40: Hineh Tov M'od
  North American Federation of Temple Youth, Union of American Hebrew Congregations.

References

Bridger, David, ed., in association with Samuel Wolk. *The New Jewish Encyclopedia.* Behrman House, 1976.
  A complete library of Jewish knowledge in one volume. A clear and concise guide to the understanding of Jewish history, thought, and civilization through four thousand years. Three hundred and eighty-nine illustrations.

Kaganoff, Benzion C. *A Dictionary of Jewish Names and Their History.* Schocken, 1977.
  Detailed discussion of the history of Jewish names and a listing of hundreds of Jewish names and their origins.

Roth, Cecil, and Wigoder, Goeffrey, Editors-in-Chief. *Encyclopaedia Judaica.* 16
volumes. Jerusalem: Keter, 1972.

A self-contained library of Judaica. A monumental achievement with brilliant full-color art, maps, diagrams, reproductions, charts, and photos. Belongs in every Jewish home.

Strassfeld, Michael; Strassfeld, Sharon; and Siegel, Richard, eds. *The Jewish Catalog: A Do-It-Yourself Kit.* Jewish Publication Society, 1973.

A fascinating mosaic of Judaica. Presents information on kashrut, Jewish
travel, the Jewish calendar, the festivals, scribal arts, music, film, and more.

Strassfeld, Michael, and Strassfeld, Sharon, eds. *The Second Jewish Catalog: Sources
and Resources.* Jewish Publication Society, 1976.

Takes up where *The First Jewish Catalog* left off, with all new material on the
Jewish life cycle, synagogue and prayer, medicine, the handicapped, education, crafts and folk art, and more. Features a 64-page supplement, "The
Jewish Yellow Pages," a comprehensive listing of services, products, and
institutions throughout the country.

Trepp, Leo. *The Complete Book of Jewish Observance.* Behrman House, 1979.

An encyclopedic guide to Jewish observance in all its richness and diver-
sity—Orthodox, Conservative, Reform, Reconstructionist, Chasidic, Ashkenazic, Sephardic. Contains sections on Jewish worship, the Jewish festivals, the rituals of the Jewish life cycle, the Jewish holidays, and Jewish
customs, traditions, and law. Describes the viewpoints of each branch of
Judaism.

Reform Judaism

Borowitz, Eugene B. *Reform Judaism Today: How We Live.* Behrman House, 1978.

What it means to be a Reform Jew today. The place of Reform in the
spectrum of Jewish belief and ritual. Is there a Reform Halachah? The un-
resolved question of Reform Judaism in the life of the Jewish state. A new
definition for the early Reform concept of the "Mission of Israel."

Borowitz, Eugene B. *Reform Judaism Today: Reform in the Process of Change.* Book 1.
Behrman House, 1978.

The impact of American democracy and Reform Judaism upon each other,
and the evolution of Reform into the quintessential American form of Jewish
life and worship.

Borowitz, Eugene B. *Reform Judaism Today: What We Believe.* Book 2. Behrman
House, 1977.

The Reform vision of God, Torah, and Israel as defined today. Can the
universal ethic of Reform Judaism's founders be reconciled with today's
concern with community and ethnicity?

Freehof, Solomon B. *Reform Jewish Practice.* Ktav, 1952.

A learned review of present-day Reform Jewish practices and the traditional rabbinic laws from which they are derived.

Some Basic Jewish Books for Your Home

Philipson, David. *The Reform Movement in Judaism.* Ktav, 1967.

    A scholarly, historical survey of the origins and evolution of the Reform movement. Considered by many to be the definitive study of the early development of Reform in Europe and in the United States.

Social Action

Vorspan, Albert. *Great Jewish Debates and Dilemmas: Jewish Perspectives on Moral Issues in Conflict in the Eighties.* Union of American Hebrew Congregations, 1980.

    Jewish perspectives on the great social debates of our time. Includes sections on Civil Liberties, Soviet Jewry, Energy and Environment, Anti-Semitism, Crime and Punishment, among others.

Soviet Jewry

Greenberg, Louis. *The Jews in Russia: The Struggle for Emancipation, 1772–1917.* Schocken, 1976.

    A scholarly presentation and analysis of the forces that shaped Jewish life in Russia, beginning with the "Haskalah" and culminating with the origins of Zionism.

Wiesel, Elie. *Jews of Silence.* New American Library, 1972.

    The author's personal account of his visit to Russia in the autumn of 1965. After visiting five Russian cities and talking to hundreds of Jews he filed this report—originally appearing as a series of articles for the Israeli newspaper, *Yedioth Ahronoth.* The result—a stirring, impassioned picture of Jewish life in the Soviet Union.

Women and Judaism

Baum, Charlotte; Hyman, Paula; and Michel, Sonya. *The Jewish Woman in America.* Dial, 1976.

    Examination of the image, as well as the reality, of Jewish women in America. Traces the adaptation to American life of successive waves of Jewish women from Germany and Eastern Europe; explores how Jewish women responded to the time and to their new culture.

Koltun, Elizabeth, ed. *The Jewish Woman: New Perspectives.* Schocken, 1976.

    A fine collection of articles about women who are powerfully drawn to feminism but who, at the same time, wish to retain and enrich their Jewish identity. Topics included are "The Life Cycle and New Rituals," "Women in Jewish Law," and "Women in Jewish Literature."

Priesand, Sally. *Judaism and the New Woman.* Behrman House, 1975.

    Intelligent discussion of the role of women in the Jewish world by America's first woman rabbi.

Zionism

Hertzberg, Arthur, ed. *The Zionist Idea: A Historical Analysis and Reader.* Atheneum, 1969.

An excellent selection of writings by Zionism's principal spokespersons with a detailed introduction by the author.

Laqueur, Walter. *A History of Zionism.* Schocken, 1976.

A comprehensive, general history of Zionism. Starts with a discussion of the European background of Zionism since the French Revolution, covers the prehistory of the movement and five decades of Zionist activities, and ends with the establishment of the State of Israel.

Polish, David. *Renew Our Days: The Zionist Issue in Reform Judaism.* World Zionist Organization, 1976.

Traces the development of the Zionist issue within American Reform Judaism, and primarily within the Reform rabbinate.

ACKNOWLEDGMENTS

I WOULD LIKE to acknowledge the many people who in so many ways have made this book possible:

—Rabbi Alexander Schindler, for his courage, vision, and ongoing commitment to reaching out.

—Edith J. Miller for her enthusiasm and constancy.

—Rabbi Erwin L. Herman for supporting my every effort since the long-ago April day I first walked into his office.

—Rabbi Lennard Thal for his wise counsel.

—Those people who read the manuscript before publication and were so generous with their insights.

—All those who have shared their lives and feelings with me.

—Ramona Souza, Eppie Begleiter, and Anita Marlais, who typed the manuscript in its different stages.

—And, most especially, I wish to acknowledge the unending support of Rabbi Daniel B. Syme, my editor, my friend. He was always there, nudging, believing, helping, caring.

LYDIA M. KUKOFF

ABOUT THE AUTHOR

LYDIA KUKOFF graduated from Beaver College in Glenside, Pennsylvania, with a degree in English literature. In 1978 she received a Masters degree in Jewish Studies from the Hebrew Union College-Jewish Institute of Religion in Los Angeles, the city where she currently resides with her husband and two children.

Ms. Kukoff, a much sought after lecturer and specialist in Jewish Adult Education, travels extensively throughout the United States and Canada. Her articles have appeared in numerous Jewish magazines and periodicals. She is a member of and program consultant to the Task Force on Reform Jewish Outreach of the Union of American Hebrew Congregations and the Central Conference of American Rabbis and sits on the Reform movement's Commission on Jewish Education. Ms. Kukoff is well known in the Los Angeles area for her directorship of a special program, "Jews by Choice: The First Years," under the joint auspices of the UAHC, the Jewish Federation-Council of Los Angeles, and the University of Judaism.